THE MILLIONAIRE VAULT FOR WOMEN

FREE Bonuses & Training Specially For You

- FREE exclusive access to life-changing materials to help you create a better lifestyle for yourself and your family.

- FREE e-books, courses and videos from some of the world's leading wealth creation experts and motivational speakers.

- FREE access to over 10+ hours of MP3 recordings of the original interviews with the millionaires in this book.

- FREE subscription to the *Millionaire Women, Millionaire You* monthly newsletter.

- FREE notifications on news and bulletins for The Millionaire Bootcamp for Women.

Register for your FREE **VIP** access now at:

www.MillionaireWomenMillionaireYou.com/vault

For every woman who dares to dream a bigger dream...

Millionaire *Women*
Millionaire *You*

How To Think, Act and Make Money
Like a Millionaire Woman

Stephanie J. Hale

www.MillionaireWomenMillionaireYou.com

Matador
5 Weir Road
Kibworth Beauchamp
Leicester LE8 0LQ, UK
Tel: (+44) 116 279 2299
Email: books@troubador.co.uk
Web: www.troubador.co.uk/matador

ISBN 978 1848763 043

British Library Cataloguing in Publication Data.
A catalogue record for this book is available from the British Library.

Typeset in 11pt Sabon by Troubador Publishing Ltd, Leicester, UK
Printed in the UK by TJ International Ltd, Padstow, Cornwall

Matador is an imprint of Troubador Publishing Ltd

Praise for *Millionaire Women, Millionaire You*

"This is a real piece of dynamite! If you are a woman and want to know the secret of becoming a female millionaire, you must read this book. Stories from 12 wanna-be millionaire women who smashed through almost every barrier to create their millionaire status and bank balance!... This book is a classic insider's guide!"
ALAN FORREST SMITH, writer & visionary, www.AlanForrestSmith.com.

"Imagine being able to pick the brains of someone who rose up from zero to millionaire. Imagine being able to grill them on every aspect of their business and life. Now imagine this with 12 women millionaires. This information is priceless."
MARK ANASTASI, internet marketer, www.mark-anastasi.com.

This book is a *Think & Grow Rich* for women. It's an amazing tool to share with others."
JONATHAN JAY, MD of SuccessTrack, www.successtrackonline.com.

"*Millionaire Women, Millionaire You* is a brilliant blueprint to keep you motivated to achieve your dreams... this book will give you an inspirational roadmap to wealth and success... No matter what business you're in, you'll get secrets that will release your financial genius and catapult you to millions!
TRACY REPCHUK, author, speaker and entrepreneur, www.WorkatHomeMomsWebsite.com.

"Ever had a sneaky suspicion that women make money differently from men? Well you were right – this book is a REAL eye-opener."
DR JOE VITALE, star of the hit movie, 'The Secret', www.mrfire.com.

"These 12 self-made women know the secrets and strategies for making millions. If you want to make money, listen up!"
LORAL LANGEMEIER, CEO of Live Out Loud and author of *The Millionaire Maker*, www.liveoutloud.com.

"*Millionaire Women, Millionaire You* is a must have... If you want to be inspired and are ready to start down your own path to millionaire status, I urge you to read these amazing stories from women who have already gone where you want to go."
ARMAND MORIN, internet marketer, www.ArmandMorin.com.

"Having a road map to success is valuable to eliminate the guesswork. Knowing how to create your first million dollars from women who have done it before you is priceless. This book is chock full of excellent advice and insights into the mindset of extraordinary women."
MELANIE BENSON STRICK, CEO Success Connections Inc.

"*Millionaire Women, Millionaire You* is a book that will captivate and inspire you... I encourage you to study each one of these millionaires and put their ideas into practice. YOU will benefit when you do!"
PEGGY McCOLL, author of *Your Destiny Switch*, www.destinies.com.

"There's no question that these women know the secrets to making millions. Each one is living, breathing proof! Learn all their secrets and take action yourself for the abundance you desire."
RAYMOND AARON, success coach & author of *Chicken Soup for the Parent's Soul*, www.GiftFromRaymond.com.

"This is an intimate look at successful women and what makes them tick. Their attitude towards life and success is a real eye-opener. If you're a woman entrepreneur or a businesswoman, this is a must read!"
MARCI ROSENBLUM, web success traffic strategist, www.websuccesstraffic.com.

"There is so much here, something of real value at every read and I recommend doing that more than once. Great reminders to follow your heart and intuition, live on purpose, be authentically you, come from love, let success find you. Emulate these women and you won't go far wrong."
JUDITH MORGAN, wealth mentor, www.JudithMorgan.com.

Contents

Acknowledgements

There are so many people to thank – friends who have generously given their time and advice – that I really don't know where to begin. I will do my best to mention everyone.

Firstly, a huge thank you to my friend and business mentor, Mark Anastasi, who taught me to think so much bigger than I ever thought possible and who kept urging me forward whenever I met a challenge.

Thanks also to my marketing mentor, Steve Harrison, at Bradley Communications who gently pointed out my shortcomings and gave me so many great ideas. Thanks to Raia King in the RTIR marketing team. Also, to the amazing Red Carpet Riders who gave support and encouragement while on their own journeys.

Thank you to Nicola Cairncross and Judith Morgan at The Moneygym; as well as the women entrepreneurs within the Mastermind Group, who patiently gave suggestions and feedback to my many questions.

Thanks to Greg Secker, Matt Shaw, Guy Cohen, Vince Stanzione, Ian Williams, Allan Kingdon, and Noel Mason for their help while I was learning to trade. Their encouragement and inspiration helped me to believe, 'I can do it'. Thanks for Greg, Matt and Guy in particular for the opportunities you gave me. Thanks to Savvas Kareklas at Inspired Group, John Harrison at Streetwise Publications and Andy Thompson at Gaia Media for sound business advice.

Thanks to Leili McKinley, Ciaran Doyle, Simon Hedley and Gareth Owen for their internet marketing expertise and for sharing this so generously. Thanks to Joanna Martin, Rosarie Nolan and Geoffrey Berwind for helping to develop my public speaking skills.

Thanks to Leigh Ferrani and Pauline Kiernan for superb writing and editing skills; to Ella Gascoigne for her PR expertise; to Aimee Fry for her creative magic; to AA Arquiza and her team for their speed and accuracy. Thanks to David Fisher and Lorraine Milligan for photography and make-up. Thanks to Jeremy Thompson and Claire Carpenter for their advice on self-publishing. It has been a real team effort. All of you have helped with an energy and enthusiasm that has been humbling.

Thanks to the kind staff at the John Radcliffe Hospital for helping me through a difficult 12 months and seeing me through to the other side of the tunnel.

Thanks to my Mum and step-Dad for your support – for being on the end of the phone when I needed you and for coming to the hospital with me. Thanks to my grandparents, long departed now, for helping to shape me into the person I am today. I miss you, but your echoes will always be with me.

The biggest thank you goes to my three children – Cormac, Tierni and Chiara – for bringing such joy and beauty into my life. I love you and I wouldn't have done a single page of this without you.

Introduction

Imagine this... your parents come to visit and there's a hooker making out with a client in broad daylight right outside your home. Or this... you're walking back from school and pass two neighbours who offer you white powder. Your son thinks they're selling sherbet. Or even this... a friend drops by and there's a wino sleeping in a pool of urine just outside your gate. Most nights you hear men fighting outside, women screaming, or cars getting smashed.

This was my life a few short years ago. Let me tell you, it wasn't a lot of fun. My car was written off by a joy rider shortly after we moved in. I lost count of the times I called the police because of violence in the street.

Believe it or not, this was a step up from my previous home. That one had water pouring in through the ceiling, toadstools the size of saucers growing in the bathroom, and green mould on most of the furniture. I couldn't hang out washing without it getting nicked. One of my neighbours even stole my credit card while I was unloading my groceries. Worst of all, a four-year-old was raped on the nearby field where I used to take my son kite flying. It was this shocking event that spurred my desire to learn about wealth creation. This was no place to bring up children.

The question I continually asked myself during these difficult years was: "How did I get here?" One minute I'd been living in a nice house, driving a nice car, leading a nice lifestyle in a nice part of the city. The next, whoomph! Pretty much overnight, I was a single mother and wondering what hit me. But the truth was I had only myself to blame.

Up to this point, I'd taken no responsibility whatsoever for my financial destiny. Saving & investment? B-o-r-i-n-g! Financial spreadsheets. You what? Monthly outgoings? Ask my husband. Truth was, I hadn't the first clue how to manage money, how to invest money, how to grow money. It just wasn't something that had been on my agenda. I'd been walking into disaster with my eyes wide shut, blindly hoping for the best. If I hadn't found this out when my marriage broke up, I sure as hell would have found out when I hit retirement age.

I spent the next few years reading everything I could get my hands on. I bought books, signed up to newsletters, attended workshops, and sought out mentors. I was working full-time, as well as evenings and weekends, to make ends meet. But in what little free time I had, all I did was study.

First, I set up my own publishing consultancy to help authors write and market their books. Then, because I knew it was important to have multiple streams of income, I learned to trade equities, commodities and Forex. I was thrilled when several years later, I was taken on as a coach at one of the UK's leading trading schools.

Things seemed to be taking a nosedive in 2008, when I was faced with a year of health challenges. But that difficult period again turned out to be a blessing in disguise. It not only prompted me to write this book, but I also co-founded The Millionaire Bootcamp for Women – and invited 10 millionaire speakers from around the world to share their top secrets and strategies with other women.

Hurdles? There have been plenty along the way. I've made stupid mistakes that have lost me money. I've placed trades that have gone belly-up. I've launched projects that have failed to make a penny. Countless times, I've felt so crushed and overwhelmed that I've wanted to give up.

High points? If you seek out help, you find it. You eventually find an answer. I wouldn't be where I am today without the kindness of mentors who were happy to share their expertise – a half-hour here, lunch there, numerous phone calls. I've learned powerful tips and strategies that would have taken me years to discover on my own. There have been the friendships I've forged with other entrepreneurs on a similar path. Every day, I've grown in knowledge and experience. Slowly, but surely, I've come to understand the principles that seemed so incomprehensible when I first heard them. Most rewarding is the awareness that I'm a role model for my three children. They too can take control of their destiny. They can one day choose a life that makes their hearts sing.

Pretty much every millionaire I've ever spoken to has a story of hardships or personal challenges overcome. Every journey has been different, yet somehow similar. It's not so much about the 'how' as the 'why'. Whatever situation you are in today, I hope this book will offer you insights and inspiration. You too can change your circumstances and lead the life you dream of. Just make the decision today. Every journey, no matter how long or far, begins with a single step.

To your success

Stephanie J. Hale

ONE

Sandy Forster

Sandy Forster is a millionaire mindset mentor, a best-selling author, an international speaker and an award-winning business owner. She was recently given the International Mentor of the Year Award for 2008. Just six years ago, she was a single mother on welfare and was $100,000 in debt.

Q: Did you always think that you would be as successful as you are today?

I wanted to be successful. I didn't even know that success was something I was achieving. But having struggled financially – having been on welfare and $100,000 in debt – I just *so* wanted to be wealthy. I wanted to be a millionaire. I just thought that I had been born into the wrong life and the wrong body. So, I absolutely wanted more. I don't think I ever imagined that I would have created the success that I have, or that I would be living a lifestyle that is so incredible and beyond

1

anything I could have imagined. So half and half: half of me absolutely wanted it, but the other half never believed that I could actually create it.

What was the single turning point in your life that turned things around for you?

I guess two incidents. First of all, I think the biggest thing for me was discovering the 'law of attraction'. I discovered that what we think about, where we put our focus, what we talk about, where we put our emotions – that is what actually creates our today and our tomorrow. So the first incident was discovering the law of attraction, and understanding that I had a say in how my life unfolded. I could actually choose to focus on what I wanted instead of how things were or how things used to be. This is what a lot of people do: they tend to create the same old thing over and over. Discovering that was a huge turning point for me.

I had been working with the law of attraction for a number of years, and I'd been going from that place of being on welfare to bringing money in. I wasn't a millionaire and I wasn't even wealthy at that stage, but I was seeing more money pouring in my life than I have ever had before. The money would come and it would go, it come it would go. Then I created an idea for a programme with a business partner – it was based on using the law of attraction as a mindset side of the programme, with practical strategies to create prosperity. This programme was called *Wildly Wealthy Women*. It was instantly a success – we had hundreds and hundreds and hundreds of women join the programme.

I remember going to the local Target store. (It was a store with a bit of everything: clothing, hardware, kids' stuff.) I remember walking down the aisle of Target knowing that I had to buy a blender, because I love making fruit smoothies in the mornings. It's my passion. I get beautiful, fresh fruit and blend it all up. It tastes so sinful that you think it's bad for you, but it's actually so good for you. That's something I love to do, but my blender had broken. So I remember going down to Target, walking down the aisle and looking at all the blenders. I was starting to look at all the prices because normally everything that I bought would be based on how much it cost. If I couldn't afford it, I wouldn't get it. So I had to always go for something that was low cost. I was looking at these blenders and suddenly, walking down the aisle, I started crying because I realised that I didn't have to look at the price. I could buy any one of those blenders that I chose. I knew in that moment – even though I didn't have hundreds of thousands in the bank – I knew that I was going to be a millionaire and that my money worries were over forever. I had opened that doorway, opened that portal if you like, to allow prosperity to flow to me forever. In that moment, it was very exciting because I knew that my life was taking a huge turn. I couldn't wait to see what would unfold.

Did you have a mentor to help you through those times? Or did you read books or home study courses? What helped you get through that initial learning curve?

I absolutely love – and I still do to this very day – learning. Obviously I couldn't afford to pay a mentor. I couldn't afford to go to live events like seminars and workshops. But I immersed myself in every book I could get hold of, every audio I could listen to. I went on every live tele-seminar I could, listened to every interview. I did everything I could that was either no cost or low cost.

Initially, two people had a huge impact on me. The first, spiritually, was Wayne Dyer. He was a wonderful mentor in really getting me to connect to my spiritual side. But then, there was also Mark Victor Hansen. He was very much someone that encouraged me to think so much bigger than I ever thought possible. He's a fabulous motivator, a great inspiration. He said that he's got ADHD – and I looked at him and thought, 'He's scattered, he's all over the place. He doesn't know what he's doing half the time. That's me!' But I looked at him and thought, 'Look at the success he's created? If he can do it, I can do it.' He really was a huge inspiration to me. So I used to read everything that he brought out. I'd race to the library and order the book if they didn't already have it. Over time, as my finances got bigger and more abundant, I then started going to his live events and buying home study courses and other things.

These days I'll buy anything, listen to anything, and attend anything that is based on success and personal development and becoming the best that you can be. I just love it. I think I'm addicted to making myself a better person.

If someone else was coming to you in a similar situation – say $100,000 in debt with two children to support – what advice would you give them?

The very first thing that people need to do is to work on a millionaire mindset. This is my absolute passion and this is what I teach hundreds of thousands of people around the world: to change their thinking when it comes to money. If they are wanting more prosperity, more abundance, more wealth, more riches in their life, the very first thing that has to change is the way they think around money. I don't mean suddenly just 'like' the idea of having more money. I mean: every thought that they have to do with money. If they see someone else with a beautiful house and a fabulous car, instead of feeling jealous, they have to feel grateful that that is actually in their life. Even if it's not theirs – it's there, they can see it, they can appreciate it. Every time a bill comes in and they can't pay it, instead of stressing and worrying about it, instead just look at it and imagine that it's paid. Write it down on a list and put a big tick against it all, or put a big cross over it all and write 'paid' next to it. Do whatever you can within your mind to create the life that you want. That will mean writing out affirmations about how you want things to be; doing visualisations and seeing that success, seeing that prosperity, seeing that abundance.

But really, that first step has to be about changing the way you think, because people either have what I call a 'prosperity consciousness' or they have a 'poverty consciousness'. The consciousness you have is not something you, or most people may even be aware of. It stems from how they were raised when it comes to money – the things they heard from their parents. Things such as: "it takes money to make money"; things such as "the rich get richer and poor get poorer"; things that you hear from the media and from business people, from well-meaning friends and family, even religion. You have all this input when it comes to money. Even now, we hear how hard times are, "the economic recession". I personally haven't bought into that and I've had the best three months that I've had for years. It's really a matter of where you want to be. Where you are now can be purely based on the fact of how you were raised around money: the things you heard, the things you buy into now. All people really need to do is change that. Instead of looking at how things are, look at how they want it to be – and they can turn that poverty consciousness into a prosperity consciousness.

It's not just changing their thinking. What happens is it changes who they are on the inside, it changes people on a cellular level. Once someone is changed at a cellular level, once they're changed from the inside out, then all the circumstances on the outside will change. If their issue is being around money, not having enough, not being able to pay bills and that's where they constantly put their focus and their attention, that's what they continue to recreate. That comes from a poverty consciousness. Instead, they need to work on changing that to a prosperity consciousness and focus on what they *would* like – success they would like to experience; the places they'd like to go to; the things they'd like to buy; the house they'd like to live in; the money they'd like to give to others. If they focus on the prosperity instead of the lack, then they will begin to change from the inside out. Once they change from the inside out, then the people and circumstances and opportunities will begin to flow into their life. This enables them to create in their reality the life that they dream of.

In your own life, you managed to increase your income from $15,000 a year to over $150,000 a year within 12 months. But then you say you lost everything again because you didn't have the money skills and the right mindset. Is that what you're talking about?

Yes, absolutely. It's the same thing we hear over and over again about people who win the Lottery and they become instant millionaires. Then two or three years later, not only have they lost everything, but they're usually worse off financially. We all stand around scratching our heads going: "Well, that's stupid. Give me the money, I'll show them how to handle it. I'll show them what can be done." But I was pretty much in the same situation. Whilst I didn't win the Lottery, I was able to create a lot of money through a new business that I'd started and the money was all pouring in. But you know what? I had not changed who I was on the inside. So, the circumstances on the outside were only temporary. So that money came in, but all these different things began occurring in my life to make it flow out again. Things would break down, things would blow up, teeth would fall out, you name it. As soon the money flowed in, it flowed straight back out again, and that's exactly what I'm talking about. You really need to change your mindset first, then create the success.

The next part of that is once you've worked on your mindset, once you're beginning to change that and create millionaire mindset, then you need to find a mentor. You need to go out into the world and know what it is that you want to do. Now at this stage you may have no idea. A lot of people say: "Yes I want to be rich, but I don't know exactly what I want to do to create that prosperity, to create that wealth." That's fine, you don't need to initially. Just find someone who *has* created prosperity and abundance, someone you resonate with, and someone whose message really speaks to you. In whatever way you can, connect with them – whether it's through going to the library and getting their books, or buying their audios, or attending one of their seminars. Just connect to their message and listen to them.

Then the third step, (once you've created your millionaire mindset, once you've found yourself a mentor) is you have to apply what you have learned. Too often in life we can get very stuck on the learning, we just immerse ourselves in finding out what to do. We *know* everything, we know all about it, but we don't actually *do* it. You see this every day of your life when it comes to people being overweight – it's nothing to do with money, but when people are overweight they usually know that all it takes is exercising more and eating less. We all know it, but is everyone doing it? No. It's the same with creating success. You can go out there and read all the books you like, you can connect with all the mentors in the world, you can attend every seminar on success. But unless you apply it, nothing is going to change.

Those three things are really key: create a millionaire mindset; find a mentor that you resonate with; and apply what you have learned.

So action is very important. Do you think this is the missing ingredient that people talk about when they say they've watched [the motivational film] 'The Secret', but they've not had any results yet?

Absolutely. The seed for making 'The Secret' occurred when Rhonda [Byrne] read the book The *Science of Getting Rich* by Wallace Wattles. It's a book written way back in 1910, so a very, very old book. However in there he says something that is very profound. He says: "By thought, the thing you desire is brought to you. But by action, you receive it." So you can sit on a mountain top and meditate until the cows come home about your million dollars, but it's not going to drop into your lap. You need to actually get out there and take action. When you spend that mindset time – that manifesting time, that metaphysical time –

imagining the wealth and putting your attention and energy and vibration there, that's the first part of the equation. But then, you have to take some action. It doesn't even matter if it's the wrong action. If it's a wrong action you'll know, and then you'll take a different action that might lead you to another step. Then that step will suddenly take you somewhere else, which will suddenly put you in connection with the right person or the opportunity or the situation that will help you. It will come in to your reality. But you have to take that action. You have to take action for it to actually appear in your life.

Action is a vital part of the missing puzzle in 'The Secret'.

You were asked to take part in 'The Secret' as one of the experts. Tell me a little about that.

Yes, that was so exciting. It's a long, convoluted story, but basically 'The Secret' was actually already out and I wasn't in it. You couldn't buy it here in Australia, believe it or not, but I managed to get my hands on a copy. I fell in love with it and really wanted to be in it – even though I knew it was already made. Previously to that, I'd heard about 'The Secret' and I'd gone on the website. I didn't have a real sense of what it was about because it was just a two-minute trailer. I remember contacting Rhonda through the website saying: "Look, I just know that what you're doing is going to transform the planet. It's going to touch billions of people. I don't know what it is –logically, I have no idea – but I just feel it in my heart. So I would love to send you a gift as a thank you." I got an e-mail back from Rhonda and she basically said: "Yes, it would be lovely. I've heard of you and your work." So I sent her my book, and she read it and loved it.

It just so happened that I was going to be in America at exactly the same place that she was, about two or three weeks later. We met up and they asked if they could film me. So they spent a whole day filming me. The plan at that stage was to bring out a series of *Secrets*. 'The

Secret' at the moment is just one DVD with a lot of different components like: the secret to life, the secret to money, the secret to relationships, the secret to health. So they were planning to bring out a series. But I think they've been so busy bringing out the initial film in many, many various languages that they haven't really got around to releasing anything else at this stage.

Would you say that was the high point of your career? Or would you say that of your book *How to be Wildly Wealthy Fast*? It jumped past bestsellers such as *Da Vinci Code* and *Rich Man, Poor Dad* – that must have been pretty amazing?

At the time it was funny because it was moving up the charts on Amazon and I just couldn't go to sleep. So I was staying up all night watching it move up, starting at around 24,000 and then moving up to 16,000 and then to 7,000 and then up into the hundreds and then up to the tens. Then it got up to number five, which is below one of Harry Potter's books. That was a wonderful, wonderful time. It was so exciting because that was early on in my career as a prosperity mentor, so that was really, really exciting. But then being selected to be filmed for 'The Secret' was a real pat on the back. Everyone that was selected for 'The Secret' was very, very well known – I'd heard of pretty much all of them. To be chosen and be recognized as one of their peers was really wonderful.

But then I think, just recently I was selected as Mentor of the Year in an international awards ceremony over in New York. That was basically women from all around the world. So to be selected as Mentor of the Year, when it was only five or six years ago that I was struggling and looking to other people to be my mentors! Here I am now transforming hundreds of thousands of lives around the world! Being awarded is fabulous. It's a beautiful, big trophy that looks like a logi sitting on my kitchen bench at home. That was really, really wonderful.

What would you attribute your success to? Some people might say: "she just struck lucky!" Would you say it's because you were prepared when luck fell in your lap or because you had a very deliberate strategy that you followed?

Gosh, that makes me laugh, "very deliberate strategy". You know what has allowed me to create my success? The fact that I usually have no idea what I'm doing and I just get an idea and I run with it. I don't think about it and I don't plan it, I just do it. If it works it works, if it doesn't it doesn't. If something doesn't work, I don't go, "oh my gosh" and spend hours and days moping about how it didn't work and what a disaster and what a waste of time. I just go on to the next great idea and implement, see what happens. I think that has really allowed me to create success. I'm very flexible. I'm very open to change. I guess I have to be because the Internet is the main part of my business. It is so fluid and constantly changing and evolving. But you can't get stuck in a rut. I guess for me that has been a huge part, the way I am just able to run with whatever idea I happen to have at the time.

But I think the second part to my success is I'm so passionate about what I do. I've been in that place of being $100,000 in debt and on welfare and it was soul destroying. I wasn't able to make simple day-to-day choices about what I wanted to do – everything was based on "did I have enough money" and the answer was always "no". I couldn't go to a yoga class because I didn't have enough money. I couldn't buy my children a bag of lollies or a packet of crisps at the store, I didn't have enough money. I couldn't let them buy from the tuck-shop at school, I didn't have enough money. I couldn't get a video, couldn't get a DVD, I didn't have enough money. All those little day-to-day choices were stripped from me and I so don't want anyone else to ever have to experience that.

I have gone from being in that real place of struggle to being a millionaire. I didn't have any support or connections, I didn't even finish high school. I don't have any great skills, I didn't have any massive amounts of knowledge. I just had a passion for helping other people to create their own millionaire mindset and the life of their dreams. I think because of that passion, that has really helped my business become successful because people get swept up in that passion. They can see that I'm so passionate about what I do, and that I really want to be an agent of change for them. They just want to be a part of it. They know that if they come on board and get swept up in that passion, and do as I invite them to do, then change will happen for them, too.

The big question is: can anyone achieve what you've achieved no matter what their circumstances?

Totally. I totally believe that. The reason I say that is because I wasn't born into this world with money. Even when I discovered the law of attraction, it didn't suddenly happen overnight. There were a lot of ups and downs. I saw an increase in prosperity and then it disappeared. Then I saw a bit more of an increase and then that disappeared. Then I saw some more and it disappeared. It would come and go – it was a bit like a roller coaster ride. So because I went through that roller coaster ride, the dips got less and the highs got a bit higher. Then the dips got less and the highs got higher. Until I got to this place where "yes, I still have my up and downs," but my life flows so much smoother and the prosperity is always there.

I teach people that. Yes, you might go through the ups and downs still and it might seem like everything is falling apart. But it's like going through a transformation just like a butterfly. It starts as a caterpillar and then becomes this butterfly, it's the same sort of thing. Don't think that just because you've discovered 'The Secret' or just because you understand the law of attraction that suddenly everything is going to fall into place. It doesn't always do that. I know that for a lot of people, it doesn't at all. They still have to go through some challenges, some hiccups, some setbacks. But they continue to create their millionaire mindset, continue to focus on what they do want, continue to see their success and abundance. When they continue to do that, then the bottom line is we're working with universal law. So, the bottom line is, it has to happen. If you continue to focus on what it is that you *do* want, the universe has to deliver. There can be no other way. It's only when you focus on what you want and how it hasn't arrived yet, it's not there and you don't think it's going to work, that the universe can't deliver. But if you continue to focus on what you *do* want and create that millionaire mindset, then it has to happen.

What motivates you? Is it your children, is it helping other people, is it the money?

Initially, it was all about the money. I was so fed up with the situation I was in, having no choices, that I just wanted the money. I don't mean 'having lots of money and spending whenever I want', I'm very much into lifestyle. I live on the Sunshine Coast in Queensland, Australia, and I love just being able to go down to the beach when I want or to have lunch with a friend or to go to a movie. It's not like I want to buy masses of jewellery, a purse, clothes and things – not that there's anything wrong with that, but that's just not who I am. For me, it was just knowing that the money would create not only financial freedom, but that it would create freedom in all other areas of my life.

So initially it was the money that motivated me. Then, it became my children. I so wanted my children to see that they can go out into the world and do whatever their heart desires. No matter what life throws at them, they have a choice and they can create their life the way they want it to be. They've very much experienced that, because they've gone from that place of never being allowed to have an ice cream when we're down the street to me taking them all over the world. We've gone to Africa and watched the wildebeest migrate across the Serengeti Plains. I've taken them to Hawaii and we've flown by helicopter over where they filmed *Jurassic Park*. I took my daughter to New York City and – because she loved the TV show *Sex and the City* – we went on a tour where they took us to Carrie Bradshaw's house and we drank Cosmopolitans at Aidan's bar. We've been to Mount Kilimanjaro and climbed to the very top. We've gone to Machu Picchu and trekked the Inca trail in Peru. The things that we've done totally transformed their day-to-day experience of life. That's what I wanted to do. I wanted to show them they could create whatever they wanted and I was a perfect example.

Now, it's about all of these things because I still love that financial freedom and I never want to lose that. So I'm always going to be motivated by continuing to make money. I always want to motivate and show my children that anything is a possible. But more than that now, it's also about helping everyone else achieve exactly the same thing because I believe if I can do it, absolutely anyone can. I know everyone is special in their own way, but I honestly don't think there's anything that special about me. I'm just like everyone else. But I totally believe that when you focus on what your heart desires and you persist, then the universe has to bring it to you.

Describe a typical day for you. How do you start your morning – do you start with visualisations, do you start by writing a list? How do you begin your day?

I love giving people the weight loss analogy because everyone can relate to that. When you're overweight and you initially want to lose weight, you have to be diligent about everything. So you have to get out the calorie counter and get out the scales. Every piece of food that you eat, you've got to measure it out and check the calories. Then you've got to exercise. You've got to keep track of what you're eating and keep track of how you're exercising. You've got to note everything, be really on top of it. That's exactly the same when you want to create prosperity and abundance.

When I first started, I would put aside an hour in the morning and it was my 'magical manifesting marathon'. In that time, I would do affirmations. I would write out my affirmation 16 or 17 times and I would see visualisations in my mind. I would read out my desired statements and I would do all the work. Then what happens over time is that you begin to be someone who's prosperous. It's the same as someone overweight who over time begins to be a healthy person with perfect weight. They no longer have to count every calorie, weigh everything they eat, or push themselves to the limit with exercise. They just make better choices every moment of every day and that keeps them at that great weight. I think that's where I am now when it comes to prosperity and abundance.

Whilst I'm going off to sleep, I make sure that I see what it is I'm wanting to create. I feel it in my heart. But I don't put aside big chunks of time to do the work – like making sure that I am visualising and doing my affirmations for so many minutes a day. It's more about doing things that make me feel good, because I know that if I feel good then I think good thoughts. When I think good thoughts, I plant the seeds of good things to happen in my life. But when I do things that don't make me feel good – like you stay up late, or if you're a drinker or a smoker, or if like me you eat too much chocolate – if I do things that I know aren't good for my body, then it makes me feel yucky. When I feel yucky, I have yucky thoughts, then I create yucky circumstances in my life, and that's how it works.

For me, I spend as much time as I can trying to do things that make me feel good then I know naturally I'm going to attract good things into my world. And because I have a millionaire mindset, I don't have to think about prosperity. I just naturally think prosperous thoughts. I naturally focus on being able to create and attract and have all those wonderful things in my world. So I don't have to put aside those chunks of time. But one thing that's really important to be able to create the life of your dreams: you need to spend a lot of time in gratitude. That means you need to focus on those things in your life that you are grateful for now.

For instance, this morning I got up at about quarter past five and I went down to the beach because I only live about six minutes from my favourite beach. As I was running on the beach, I was just so grateful for living in that part of the world and the beautiful weather, to be able to watch the waves come in. Was I focusing on abundance and prosperity and wealth? No, but I was focusing on things that made me feel wonderful. What that does, that puts an energy or a vibration or an order out into the universe to attract more things that make me feel amazing and wonderful and fabulous. So, if people can spend more time being in that place of gratitude, then they'll notice that naturally over time they will begin to attract more things into their world that make them feel even more grateful.

Then when they're even more grateful and they're noticing all those great things, then they're even more in that vibration and energy. Then they place more orders for the same things, and then they attract even more. So, it's this wonderful cycle. Instead of cycling down it's cycling up, attracting these wonderful things in your world simply by being grateful. Being grateful for what you already have can create so much more in your world.

You see gratitude in children, and that wonder and awe when they're very small. Then it slowly disappears as people get older. Why do you think that happens?

Unfortunately when it comes to society, all the institutions that are there supposedly to help us seem to knock the daylights out of us. Places like school, for instance, if someone was sitting in the classroom and they're daydreaming about something amazing and wonderful and great, they would get wrapped over the knuckles and asked to concentrate. If they were told to write out an essay about something that they wanted to have in their world, if it was too big and too grand, they'd be told, "Don't be stupid, you couldn't do that. You couldn't have that." I'm not saying anything against teachers, because my sister is a teacher. But it's very much the actual institution itself. School, and the media knock the expectations out of people. They try to bring everyone back to reality.

Sometimes even friends and family do the same thing – not because they're wanting to hold you back or they don't want you to experience success – but they think that if you don't reach this wonderful life that you want to create, you're going to be so disappointed. So rather than let you get into that space, they'll pull you back and tell you all the reasons why it won't work now, before you even try, so that you won't get disappointed. Now in reality, how stupid is that? But that's pretty much the way we work, that's the way we're raised. That's the way society teaches us. But if we could just let all that go and instead begin to be that child again: begin to wake up each morning with the anticipation for what's going to happen, what we're going to attract into our world today, what amazing things are going to unfold. If we can start each day like that, we can bring amazing things into our world each day. We need to get back to that child-like excitement and anticipation for our life, rather than the: "Ho-hum, here I go. Off to work again, how dull." That's what sort of really extinguishes the spark of manifesting in most people.

Tell about some of your clients – what makes people come to see you in the first place? What makes them go outside of their comfort zone? Is it because they've had a crisis in their lives or something 'big' happens?

I think it's very much a cross-section. A lot of people are drawn to my message simply because they have a yearning in their soul for something more. They know that the life that they're living is not necessarily the one that makes their heart sing. They know that they should be doing something or experiencing something or going somewhere. Their life should not be the way it is at the moment. When they hear me speak, rather than just talk about facts and figures and 'let's make money', they hear that the way I create prosperity is more about connecting to the spiritual self. It's more about sending orders out to the universe than, "ok, let's work so many hours a week." I think that really resonates with a lot of women. They love the idea that they don't need to be some sort of brain surgeon to go out there and create more success and prosperity in their world.

They just need to 'get' and understand at a really deep level what universal law and the law of attraction is all about. They need some simple strategies to use in their day-to-day life, and then to combine that with practical strategies, and so that the prosperity will begin to flow. It may not be in a tidal wave the first week. But it will begin to come in drops, it will begin to turn into a brook, it will turn into a river. It will get bigger and bigger. I think that's why people are drawn to me because it is that message of joining the practical with the metaphysical. The two together are what creates their success. People know they want something more, though they don't necessarily know what that is. So they're drawn to my message because it just resonates with them.

If I had to go out and take a practical first step today, what would you suggest that I do as the most effective thing in the next 24 hours?

I'd give you a 'mindset step' and a 'practical step'. So the mindset step would be: spend 15 minutes today and imagine that you just won the Lottery. Just for 15 minutes, write down everything you'd do: the places you'd go, the things you'd experience, all the toys that you'd buy, whatever it is that makes your heart sing, the people that you'd help. Write down whatever it is that sets you on fire. Don't write it down from the space of "Oh my gosh, how much is that? Am I going to be able to afford it?" No, you've just won the Lottery and for all you know the prize was $30 million. Don't write it down from a logical level, write it from a place of feeling.

Instead of just writing "I'm going to Egypt," *feel* what it would be like to actually be in Egypt. Have that hot sun shining down on your skin, feel that hot breeze blowing through your hair. See yourself going up to the great pyramids, touch them and feel that roughness, smell the smells that you'd smell when you're in Egypt. Feel your foot taking that first step up those huge pyramids and flood your body with the joy and excitement. Look at the people that are with you – maybe you've taken your family or your lover or your best friend or your children – look at their faces and feel how proud you are that you've been able to create this and have them be a part of that experience. When you write it all out, get into the feeling place because your feelings are what create. It's not the writing it down, it's not saying the affirmation, it's not reading out the desire statement, it's the feelings. The feelings are what send that order out to the universe and allow the universe to bring it back to you. So write down this ideal, amazing, fabulous life that you're creating now that you've won these multi-million dollars and get into the feeling place of that. That's the first thing that you could do.

Then the practical step I would say is start saving your coins. What I mean by that is: I never spend a coin. No matter how expensive or inexpensive something is – even if it's 20 cents – I always pay with paper money. I take all my coins and I put them in a little jar, then when that jar's full I put it in the bank. You might say: "Why do you bother doing that now?" It's a habit that I got into when I had no money whatsoever. What I found out was I had a finite amount of money coming in each week, and when I made the decision that I wasn't going to spend my coins, I would put them in the bank instead. What this did was it stopped me from making choices about spending, because I obviously had less money because I was amassing these small coins. Not that I used to overspend, because I didn't have money to overspend, but you'd be surprised at what happens. I didn't buy that chocolate bar for myself because I didn't want to break a note, I wanted to put these coins aside.

Then what happened is that I was beside myself with joy the very first time that I put those coins in the bank. I think it added up to about $198 – and that was the first time that I actually had money in the bank in an account that I was not going to touch. My plan was to keep putting money in there and then take money and do something with it – whether it was to pay money off my credit card or eventually put that money into something that would multiply. The plan was just to have money. From a metaphysical perspective, that did amazing things for me. Believe it or not with $198, I suddenly felt rich. I actually had money saved up, and for me that was a huge thing.

For people that may be in a position now where they are struggling, try not to spend any coins. Put them in a jar. When the jar is full, take them to the bank. As that money accumulates, make a plan for that money. That may be as simple as: I'm going to take that money and I'm going to do nothing but put that down on my credit card debt, I'm going to pay it off that way. You'd be amazed at the difference that it could make. It makes a difference not just on a practical level but on a metaphysical level as well.

So, those are the two tips that I'd be giving people.

Can you tell me about some of the people that you've helped over the years, some of the success stories of lives that have been transformed?

It's been incredible. I just love getting e-mails and letters from people. I remember one lady e-mailed me to say that she had been in a car accident about a year earlier. She'd fractured her spine in three places, she was in the hospital for months, and she was really depressed. She tried to commit suicide a number of times because she was really struggling financially and in every other area. Her life was totally falling apart.

She came across a book that I was in. From that book and reading a bit about me, she jumped on my website www.wildlywealthywomen.com and saw that I offer a lot of free things: free tele-seminars, free e-books and audios, etc. So she took a lot of the free things I had and then her life started to change. The next thing you know, she became a published author with me in one of my compilation books. Then she went out there and started writing articles. Now, it's about 18 months later, she has a very successful business and writes articles for a number of online article banks. She's published two or three books of her own. She has a website where she helps other women to create their own prosperity, abundance, and success. She has totally transformed her world.

Now, this is someone who was suicidal. This is why I say to people: "Look, we're talking universal law here. If you apply what it is that I teach, if you create your own millionaire mindset, then anything is possible. You have no excuse because it is universal law." So if someone who is suicidal can transform their life in less than 18 months, then all it really takes is an idea. It takes the right mentor and it takes applying what you learn. Anything is possible.

Do you think it's important to have a team around you to help you with the changes – even if it's just, for example, a web designer or a copywriter?

Absolutely. At the start, I know for me personally, I did it all. I couldn't afford to hire anyone else; I couldn't afford to get someone to help me. Now, obviously I have quite a few people on my team, but I love virtual assistants. I have about six or seven virtual assistants – only one of them lives here in Australia. The rest of them live in Canada and America. I've never met them; I probably never will meet them. It's lovely being able to say to someone, "Can you change this in my website" or "I need this form made" or "Can you contact that person?" These are usually moms that work from their own homes. They work on an hourly rate, so you only pay them for what they do. They're not on full-time. You don't have to pay them every week; you don't have to pay them sick pay or holiday pay. You give them a task, they do it and they just bill you for the hours that they work. That's something that every person will need to look at, if they're wanting to create huge success.

But this is a real key – before you get to the place of hiring anybody, start to write down what you do every day. If you do a particular task, detail it, write a flow chart, have a checklist. You might think, 'Why do I need that? I'm the only one that's doing it!' Let me tell you from experience: I used to do everything, and I mean *everything*. I did the marketing, I did the website, I set the tele-seminars up, I recorded things. I did everything myself. I got to the point where I was so busy doing all the work, that the idea of actually *telling* somebody how to do the work on top of *doing* the work was overwhelming. It took me years to hire somebody to do something simply because training them to do it seemed so daunting. But now, every time someone does something in my business, I tell them: "You do a flowchart, do a checklist." This is so that whenever anyone else needs to do it, no one needs to be told anything, We just give them a piece of paper and they follow the step-by-step instructions.

You definitely need a team of people that are going to assist you if you plan on creating huge success, and I just don't mean a business team. I have someone that comes in who cleans my house; I have someone that mows my lawn; I have someone that does my pool; I have someone that landscapes my garden. I'm looking at getting someone to come and prepare healthy meals for me. In fact this week, I've just found an organic gourmet food service. They prepare meals and deliver them to your house. It's lovely being able to do that now, because financially I'm in a position to do it.

There's certain things you can do that will make all the difference. For instance, when I was struggling financially, one of the things that made me feel rich beyond my wildest dreams was getting my house cleaned. So once every two weeks, I would get someone in for an hour and a half and it cost me around $25. So that would work out to around $12.50 a week, to get someone to clean my house. I loved it. When they left, I felt rich. I felt so sparkling clean, so fresh and new, and it made a huge difference. Even if you're not financially in a position to get support all the time, just try and do something somewhere in your life. Again, from a practical standpoint, it will really help. But from a metaphysical standpoint, it will help you to connect with that person who is financially free with all the support they need.

Your plans for the future… what are your plans for the next five to 10 years?

Ten years is way too far out, I'm a plan-next-week type of person. I've just recently launched InspiredSpiritCoaching.com. That's a programme where I train people to be coaches. I train them to use all of the principles in *How to Be Wildly Wealthy Fast* so they can create their own business and transform people's lives. I figured I can't do it all on my own, so I put together a coaching academy that trains people so that they can have a lot of fun transforming people's lives but at the same time create a wonderful income for themselves.

What sort of age range would you say your clients are?

The youngest I can recall was 17 – at one of my seminars. That's not to say that I don't have people younger than that because I know a lot of moms say: "My daughter or my son uses the principles in your book and they're getting so much value from them. They got high marks at school and they've got the job that they want." So I know there are younger kids too. When it comes to the target range that utilises all my products, it's very much women in the 30-55 age group. They're the ones that really get the most out of it. Women whose their souls are yearning for more and they just want to create an amazing, wonderful life.

More information at: www.wildlywealthywomen.com

TWO

Jennifer Hough

**Jennifer Hough is President and founder of The Vital You, the
largest holistic nutrition clinic in Canada. She is co-creator of Soul
Awakening Adventures – with retreats to Peru, Sedona, Bali,
Bimini Bahamas and Costa Rica. She transformed her own life
from years of financial struggle and chronic migraines to one of
abundance and limitless vitality. When she first set up her
business, she had no desk and no office, so would hold
consultations sitting cross-legged on her living room floor.
Jennifer is also a bestselling author, speaker and radio show host.**

Q: Tell me about the early days of your business. What led you to set
it up and how did you get things going?

I graduated from Waterloo University with a degree in economics and
sociology. When I graduated, and instead of following my heart, I
actually did what I was *supposed* to do, I got every job I applied for and

fell into the job that everybody wanted. I suspect that was mostly personality. After graduating, I had the chance to live in Quebec and learn French, go overseas and learn Spanish. But Proctor & Gamble wanted me to come and work for them and join their team. My heart said: "go and learn a new language" and my logical mind said: "Jennifer, you've got a great job opportunity, it's got benefits, it's going to last a long time. Their training is incredible, do that." So, I actually started corporately and I received great training over the years with Proctor & Gamble and it was wonderful.

One of the great things about my life is that my heart and my purpose-calling is so powerful. I didn't know what it was; I didn't even know I was off-purpose. You'll love this: I was in a middle of a performance review and my lovely manager Jocelyn was interviewing me. I remember to this day. She said: "So Jennifer, you are good at this, good at that." Then, she started using all these acronyms that we do in corporate speak. I'm like: Oh my God. My eyes started twitching, my head started twitching. She said: "Are you okay?" I replied: "Yes, I'm fine. I'm fine." All of these confining words: instead of something being a real pain in the butt it was "a challenge"; instead of something being a total problem it was "an opportunity". I said to myself, "Oh my gosh, this doesn't feel real to me." That was just the feeling I was having. Right in the middle of my performance review – which was half decent, it was probably a B plus performance review – I said: "Jocelyn, I have to leave." She said, "Do you have to go to the bathroom?" And I said, "No. I mean I have to leave Procter & Gamble." She said: "Do you have an appointment?" I said: "No. Actually, I think I'm quitting."

Up to that point, it had never crossed my mind to leave. Ever. Not once. It just occurred to me in that moment because I was wide open to something more. It occurred to me that I was listening to something that I hadn't listened to before. It had probably been building for so long that it took a performance review to have it burst open. Something greater was calling to me.

Did you know what you were leaving *to* at that time?

I had no flipping clue. I had no idea. I just knew that something more was calling me. Now I had done something called "implementing total quality," I had facilitated that. I facilitated some other programmes having worked in purchasing and negotiating. It was wonderful and I loved doing that. So I was facilitating and doing workshops already in my mid-twenties. That was pretty exciting and confidence building, so before long I became a business consultant. I worked as a sales manager for an art company. That was all fine and good, but I knew it was totally off-purpose. My first step was that I needed to be free of the group mentality. I needed to be myself. So being an entrepreneur allowed me to be myself, to actually hear myself.

I've got to tell you, one of the most meaningful processes I've ever been through is the process of being free. This was me doing something that was somewhat creative, something I knew that I could do – so kind of brainless, somewhat easy for me – so that I could actually just *be* for long enough to hear my thoughts and feelings. So for a year and a half I did that, maybe two years. I lived on my sailboat, and in that time I caused myself to be $30,000 in debt.

That must have been quite scary at the time – how did you feel?

Thirty thousand dollars in debt for someone being half-commission paid, also self-employed, looking for customers, and really having very little experience being an entrepreneur, was *very* scary. The mistake I made, I went, "Oh my gosh, I've got to calculate where all this $30,000 debt is coming from," so I itemized it out. A lot of what I'm going to share with you is going to be backwards from some advice that other people might give. I itemized all of the things and all the places where I owed money. What I did is I posted it on a piece of paper. I thought I was being a responsible Canadian girl. I posted it on the door of the loo so I could see it as I was leaving the boat every day. What an appropriate place to put that piece of information! I would go up the stairs on the sailboat and I would see all of these items where I owed money. You know, $2,000 here, $5,000 there, and $10,000 there, a lot of money. Of course every day before I left the boat, I figured that would actually motivate and inspire me to get into action. Actually, what it did was it just kept reminding me of how powerless and how underneath it all I was.

There came a point – and it was quite an epiphany – because it didn't only happen in the area of money, it also happened in the area of my relationship. It was sort of like an opening up of everything. It was like a major, major "aha". I got up, (and this has happened to me several times since then by the way) and I had an awakened dream. I literally sat up at about two or three in the morning, and I saw the common denominator in the mess that was being created. My relationships seemed to be the same relationship over and over again. Actually, you'll find this hilarious, they were so much the same relationship over and over again that the three guys I had dated previous to this "aha" moment were *all* named Ian. Not only was it the same pattern, it was the same guy. In the financial place, I was sort of being Pollyanna: "it'll all be okay, tomorrow I'll work harder." All that kind of stuff. When really, it was all because I wasn't living my purpose; nor was I doing that in my relationships. It was time to move on and find what I was put on this planet for.

What happened after that?

What happened after that is I found pockmarks in the bottom of my sailboat which I had to refinish. I got extremely sick, and I could have died from the exposure I had. As a result, I ended up meeting someone in my chiropractor's office who taught me about nutrition. We exchanged services: I helped her with her business and she helped me with nutrition. I read a little book called *Eating Alive*. I had migraines, I had depression, and I had welts up and down my neck. As a result of that health crisis that happened right after this little "aha" moment, I changed my entire situation of well-being. Prior to that health crisis I had my biological age tested, my cellular age. At 28 years old, my biological age was 42. Now I'm 43 years old, almost 44. I had my biological age tested last year (which was at 42) and my biological age was 31.

Great. Gosh, that's amazing.

Two-thirds of my symptoms got better within four or five months of changing nutrition, changing my health protocol, etc. All of my friends started asking me: "What are you doing?" I was a personal trainer at that time, by the way. For 10 years I've been a personal trainer and an aerobics instructor. I did that on the side because, why not get paid for doing exercise? All of those people started saying: "Jennifer, my God, you look *amazing*. What happened to you?" So I started teaching them the nutritional principles that I had learned. Before long, I was doing way more nutrition than anything else. Before long, my nutrition practice had found me. I didn't invent it.

So you started out very, very small and you were trying lots of different things. You were doing fitness and you found that nutrition was increasingly taking more of your time. Did you have a mentor during those years?

What I had was the mentor of following my heart – literally waking up every morning and saying: "What feels good to do now?" I did find a mentor in a woman named Corolla Barzak. She had such a passion for assisting people through physiology, biology, etc. My mentor was not so much in the business sense, as it was in the following your passion and coming from love and assisting people. The more I came from love and assisted people, because of how much what I learned had helped me, the more people could see the authenticity. I have an absolute adoration for helping people wake up their bodies so that their bodies can support them in their dreams. That was very clear to me right from the get-go. That's why I was doing what I was doing.

So authenticity then, you think is very important?

Yes, authenticity is the key. You must be true to how you feel and follow your heart. Unless, of course, your passion is money. That works. If your passion is making money and you're really passionate about making money, if that's your passion. But if what you do is make sweaters and you start to make it about: "how much money can I make?" When you started out making really beautiful sweaters, people could see the love that was poured into them. When you compromise quality for quantity, that's when things go askew.

It's about having an emotional connection, an empathy with your clients or your clientele?

It's about evolving your gifts and then passionately communicating them to the world. Each of us came from billions of people who came before us. Those billions of people who came before us have launched through their yearning for a better world, a time like now, where a better world is possible. You not living your purpose, or you not living your gift, is to literally take away your piece of the puzzle from the expansion of a world where we all can get along. Even if it's making sweaters, or if it's nutrition. Actually what I do now isn't exactly nutrition, I'll share with you a little bit if you want. I'll share with you how my business grew so big.

Yes, that would be great.

Definitely, the fundamental piece of it is this: instead of listening to my head, listening to my heart. I made my husband mental because he's the President of an equestrian goods company and his life is all about strategic plans, etc. Now he's changed a lot since marrying me.

But he was very frustrated with me at the beginning, because I would not do a strategic plan. I wouldn't.

That was going to be my next question: did you have a strategic plan?

I can tell you that I had a – let's call it a divine cosmic plan. We'll say I had a dream for how many people I wanted to assist, and for how I envisioned people feeling from having worked with me. So I did have a vision, but it wasn't so specific really.

So a lot of it came from your heart?

It came from developing the skill of listening to something that went far beyond the confines of my university understanding of life.

At what point did you become confident that your business was going to be a success and that you weren't going to have to worry about the $30,000 that you owed?

You'll laugh because when I first started in nutrition, I'd just met Gary (that was my husband at the time). We lived in a tarpaper shack and I had pink shag carpet and no desk. People would come to our little one room place, I would sit on the pink shag carpet and we would have our consultations sitting on the floor. It's almost like it had mystique, because they started referring people and truly I was out in the middle of nowhere. This is a little place called Uxbridge – an hour away from humanity – and people would drive all the way to Uxbridge. So I knew I was on to something, but I was tippy-toeing because I was in debt.

By the way, the $30,000 in debt, what happened when I was in the boat after the epiphany – yes I did get sick and all of those things, but another crazy thing happened. That was that I literally surrendered what I thought I knew about how I needed to make the money. I cried – it was like: "I can't do it." Two days after I did that, I got a contract with Kentucky Fried Chicken of all things. Pretty funny that, considering I was going to be a nutritionist later – my saviour! The 'be all, end all' that got me out of debt was Kentucky Fried Chicken! I got a contract for $20,000. So that was step number one of listening to my heart.

Then came step number two which was: okay, now I need to take care of myself. I need to notice when people start talking to me about what it is that I've done with my life and what has changed my life. When people start talking to me, instead of, "Yes, it's been really good. Here, read this book," it's, "Hey, wait a second, I'm on to something here. People actually want to come and see me about this." It's going with the flow of what's presenting. What's presenting is people want to see me about nutrition because I'm an example and I'm very passionate about it because of how it changed my life. So, me becoming a nutritionist was a really a natural evolution of just looking at what was presented to me, and then following the natural flow of that. All of a sudden, here I am on a pink shag carpet, which led to having an office and eventually led to having an assistant.

Now, one might wonder at the evolution of that, to get to a place where I'm teaching *Get Out Of Your Own Way*. It seems like it's a far cry from giving people cleanses, and taking wheat out of their diet, to teaching *Get Out Of Your Own Way*. Quite frankly, the time that I knew that I was on to something is after a very sick client came in. It saddened me because I knew she was going to pass away. I was still suffering once a month from migraine, so I wasn't all the way better myself. It was about six or seven years into my career. This woman came to see me. She was lovely and she had given up. Even though her words were, "I came to see you because I want to get better," her energy was "I came to see you because I just want to know whether I'm going to be okay when I die." It just struck me because I knew that she had children and a husband that loved her; it just struck me that I wanted to be a party to something different. I want people to not only survive,

I'm interested in people who are *living* their lives. Living, truly living, wide open, wide awake. That actually transcends calling themselves cancer survivors, and so they start calling themselves wide open livers and lovers of life, where cancer doesn't even come in to the picture.

That night, again I woke up between two and three in the morning. I also had a lot of migraine suffering clients like I was, and I thought, 'I'm going to do it'. I started writing and I didn't stop for five hours. I came up with an entire programme to assist my clients and myself with a protocol to transcend the belief systems that had created the biochemistry that led to the illness. I called that programme *Get Out Of Your Own Way*. Because what had happened was when I started as a nutritionist, I didn't have any teachers aside from Corolla. She didn't teach me how to actually have a practice and put together an assessment. So I invented that all myself. One of the things I invented was a timeline analysis where I looked at my clients' physiological health. Right underneath it, I was examining their emotional well-being.

When I put those two timelines together, what I would notice is patterns of trauma that happened in their life that would lead to belief systems to keep themselves safe or to make themselves right or to protect themselves from falling again or whatever it was. Those belief systems, very specific ones, were connected to very specific physical symptoms. So, that led up to that night where I woke up, and I started thinking, 'How do I actually assist people in remembering that they are totally unlimited and that they are not a function of their traumas? They are free to create their lives and be in connection to something much greater than them. They're in connection to life and they don't need to protect themselves from life, because life wants to support them. How do I get people to connect on that level?' So, this technique came out of that wonderful lady who did eventually pass away. I sort of dedicate the technique to her because she really was the catalyst for *Get Out Of Your Own Way*. When I developed that program, that's when I knew this is why I was put on the planet. This is why I'm here. That's how it evolved.

Now we're working on projects to bring to the forefront children who are doing extraordinary things in the world. The capacity they have when they tell their stories, the innocence and the purity just reaches in to that part of you that remembers how easy life can be and how you can make a difference. It just resonates so powerfully with that part of you that you don't even need to go into the analysis or looking at the beliefs. It's like, "Oh my God! Yes, I remember."

In the early days, how did people find out about you? You mentioned that you're living out miles away from anywhere. How did people get to find out about you? Was it through the Internet, through direct marketing, direct mail or word-of-mouth?

I don't know if I'm unusual to the other stories, but my business was developed entirely on making a difference in people's lives and them telling other people.

So, through word-of-mouth then? It must have been very powerful word-of-mouth.

It was a very powerful experience people were having. At some point after that, people would bring me into their homes and bring their friends over. I would go to their homes and I would do an evening session, and I did that for a few years. Again, it wasn't a brilliant marketing idea. It was people telling me that I needed to do that. My life has literally presented itself to me and I followed life. As opposed to: I went to a textbook and I did the brochure and then I decided to get an e-mail list. Instead of me knowing about it first and going "I should do that", it presented itself to me. Then I jumped on it, because I know that when life presents me something, it's time to say "yes". So if I was to put my strategy of business success into a nutshell, it's say "yes". Say "yes" to what presents, until it's a "yes" in another direction.

Is that the advice you'd give to somebody who is setting up their own business now, somebody who's just starting out?

I actually do business mentoring, I teach a course called *The Holistic Practitioner Mentorship Course*. It's teaching practitioners how to develop a business very much based on the model that I used to build my business. It's based on making a difference with people first, and then developing all the other tools afterwards. What you need first is you need to have an income so you can get food on your table and have a roof over your head. What you need to do first is sometimes things that may be along the lines of working in a health food store in the case of a holistic practitioner. Work in a health food store for $10 or $11 an hour, while you're doing the other stuff. The first step I always say is find your niche. Find who it is you love to work with, or what it is you love to do within the realm of the career you've chosen. For instance, I love to work with women who put everyone else first and not themselves. That's my niche. My niche is women who don't say "no". They're too busy saying "yes" to everybody else.

That's a lot of women!

Yes, it is. That's my niche. The niche actually revealed itself. I started to notice who was coming to see me. It was all women who said: "I don't have time, I feel like I'm living everyone else's life. I'm a little depressed. I feel like I'm gaining weight, I'm not taking care of myself." All of these things were presenting. I thought, 'My God, what is that niche? Those are all women who don't say "no". Great, that's my niche – women who don't say "no".'

Finding that 'niche' would be the first step. The way that I show people to find that is: firstly, it has to be a group of people you love working with. Secondly, make sure that you've surrounded yourself with a great team of like-minded people. You love working with them, it's really fun for you. Thirdly, the clientele that you attract are people that have the capacity to pay you. They actually can pay you. There are niches that people love to work with, but the people don't have the capacity to pay. If they can't pay, ask yourself can it be sponsored, and by who?

Another criteria for finding that niche for me, is that it's really important that a niche exists in the media, so you can find them. For instance, a women's television programme or a women's magazine, and you know they're writing articles about women who do too much like wonder women, superwomen or super moms or whatever. So you're looking for a place that if you wanted to advertise, there are places that exist. But the biggest thing for me is you know the niche exists because people are writing about it. These people are findable. That's a really important point, too.

Did you advertise in the early days of your business? Did you do much advertising?

Not at all. Zero. None. All word-of-mouth.

So how long was it before you did any advertising?

It took me four years before I was doing the little events at people's homes. But again, it was people asking me to do them. It wasn't because I pursued. I didn't have any brochure on me doing events at people's houses. Again, that came to me. I have never paid for an ad in a magazine. I've always written articles in magazines, so that's a form of promotion, publicity and advertising. That's a great way to share information and get the word out to women that my words resonate with. I love writing. People were beginning to watch for my articles. I was asked to write a couple of articles in lifestyle and women's magazines and I realized this is a great way of getting the word out there, and I started writing for a few more magazines. So that was one of the first ways that I started to officially promote my business. Another way was I started a newsletter called *The Great Life E-News*. When I started *The Great Life E-News*, I wanted to give people very actionable things, pragmatic things: how do I wake up to who I am today, and what recipes can I use for food, inspiring stories and stuff. I did those once a month. I've been doing this for 17 to 18 years now, so I started taking that inspired action more than 10 years ago.

Pretty interesting evolution! Watch what presents. Another way that I market my practice is – again, like non-advertising – it's called SOUL mails, *SOUL E-wakenings*. Every day I get up, and just like I did with those wakened dreams for lack of a better way of saying it, I meditate and come up with an idea every morning that is like an awakened, juicy, life-changing message that's less than a few sentences long. These *SOUL E-wakenings* go out every morning online and are absolutely free. They go to thousands of people all over the world.

People can sign up for those from your website?

Yes. The last one was, "Maybe if the entire universe is your co-pilot – all-seeing, all-knowing, blah blah blah – it's time for you to change seats." The one before it was, "Intention is something to give your mind to do while you higher self is working out your magnificent life. Your mind doesn't have to know what you want for your life to show up miraculously. In fact, your brain thinking it knows what you want generally limits the outcome." Then there's a little blurb that goes underneath, and I send those out. At the bottom of the e-mail, usually there are a couple of announcements of an upcoming courses tele-workshops, seminars, soul adventures and lots more. The body of the *SOUL E-wakenings* is this inspired free message that I do every morning.

You mentioned that women are saying 'yes' and are overstretched. Do you think that men and women have different challenges when it comes to making money?

Oh my gosh, yes. Oh yes. First of all, there are the brain differences between men and women. Women multi-task and they get ingrained very early that they're responsible for everything going well. It's kind of like: if I don't do it myself, it's not going to get done right. It's just like being responsible for a household, being responsible for the kids, also having a job. Our brains have the capacity to do that – so we do. Men on the other hand are very linear and can focus on doing one task at a time and do it very, very well. Also, to be a boy is to be encouraged to be competitive and to like to play the game, to see how you can win the game. For women, it's like: how can everyone get along and how can we make this, for lack of a better word, ecological. It's very different from men to women because women's culture is to try to be as ecological as possible. Men's culture in business is to figure out how to compete, how to win. So they're two very different cultural focuses when it comes to making money.

Now the interesting thing right now is the feminine is really being brought into our economic situation. We're having to figure out a way in the current economic times to learn how to be more harmonious. So the feminine is actually being drawn into the economy. The more naturally 'woman's way' of being is a little more encouraged, because it's the only way many of us are going to survive.

Would you say men and women have a different approach when it comes to business – setting up a business or operating a business?

For sure, yes. Of course to say "yes" and give you a pat answer would be to vastly generalize – because there's some men that operate in a sort of feminine realm, and there's some women who are really like 'go get 'em tiger' kind of people. The way the female physiology is designed (I know this having been a nutritionist) is literally on the most basic level to procreate. One of the fundamental design elements of someone that's meant to procreate is that we have to be sensitive enough – in other words intuitive enough – to be able to protect the unborn child. We're designed to be very, very intuitive, to protect, and to read what's going on around us all the time, even if you never plan or experience giving birth.

So in the set up in the running of a business, women tend to be a bit more sensitive to how everybody is doing. The other thing is women definitely need to take time out to take 'me time'. Men can be like work horses. Men can just be linear and go. They have the physical capacity to do that – the biological capacity, I don't mean the physical strength. Literally, their biology would support that. Women are so sensitive that running a business has to be a lot different. There has to be balance, there has to be consideration for if everyone else is balanced. Balance is very important in feeling good and feeling like you're supported. The biggest thing for women is feeling like you're appreciated, and feeling like other people are being appreciated. That's a huge cultural thing for women, making sure that they appreciate themselves and that they're also appreciating others, and that's part of the culture of the business.

What about attitude towards money? Is there a gender difference with attitude towards money?

What I can speak of is in the holistic health world and naturopathic doctors and nutritionists. I don't know if you've noticed this, but have you noticed how weird holistic practitioners get about money?

No, I haven't.

I'm telling you, it's a cultural, bizarre thing, and most of them are women. Women tend to have a lot of problems asking for money.

They do. Because we're so used to doing so much for so many for nothing. It's only our perception that it's for nothing, because in all honesty we get love, we get connection. We're paid back in so many ways if we don't just look at the money component. We're paid back far more than money could ever pay us. There's a belief around money that, 'shouldn't I be doing this out of the goodness of my heart?' Listen, you can't do it out of the goodness of your heart, if you don't have a house and food.

It reminds me of one of my clients. Her name is Helen. She said to me: "Jennifer, I'm embarrassed about how much money I make." They're millionaires. She said: "I really don't want to let people know that I have these beautiful things and this beautiful house, and I'm embarrassed. I'm Catholic, I feel guilty." I said: "Helen, there are people out there like Donald Trump who unabashedly have tons of money, and he just flaunts it and he has no problem with it whatsoever." Now, I don't hold anything against Donald Trump for having lots of money. But I mean in the world of people that care and are going to do amazing things with their money and make a difference, wouldn't I rather have Helen be the one with that much money rather than him? Do you know what I mean?

Nothing against Donald Trump, he can make all the money he wants. But if I had the choice between Helen having it and him having it, I know what she's going to do with it. So, it's just getting over that weird cultural thing of 'it's bad to have'. It's not bad to have. You can do amazing things. Who better to have than the half of society that so naturally thinks with their heart – and there are many men that think with their heart, too.

What would you say then is the biggest roadblock to success?

For women? It's not trusting their intuition. Listening to the book and the people outside of themselves, rather than actually listening to the call of their heart. Listening. Knowing that their heart is God's megaphone. Who better to believe than omnipotence? You're a cosmic support team. The biggest block definitely is not trusting your instinct and not being able to trust what your heart is telling you.

You took quite a big risk when you left your job. How big or small do you think the risk should be that other people take? Or again, is it a matter of just listening to their hearts and their intuition?

I think listening to your heart or your intuition is the best way, because for me I knew I would be okay. If you don't know that you're going to be okay, you want to do the work so that you know you're going to be okay, *then* make the jump. It could be simply doing a spreadsheet to see the minimum you need to make, how much per hour, so that you can get out of where you are so that you'll have the brain freedom to listen to your heart and then take the next steps.

Often entrepreneurs are told to find out what their purpose or passion is. But once they've done this, how do they go about monetizing their passion? For example, I can think of people who like stained glass or canoeing, what is the next step for them?

To actually monetize what their purpose is? The cool thing is that there are so many of us out there teaching how to monetize that. Oftentimes, the biggest missing step is even knowing that you can. Knowing that it's possible, knowing that there's nothing wrong with you, knowing that you were here for a purpose. The other piece of it is allowing it to present, rather than trying to adopt the model from a textbook that fits some people and doesn't fit others.

Marketing is evolving such that it's becoming much more honest and much less creating the sense of urgency and a 'limited time offer' and a 'free extra gift', that kind of stuff. We're definitely changing how we're marketing things and just allowing those types of models to present. I think it's really about not reinventing the wheel as well. It's allowing your own system of doing things to evolve using other people's models to formulate what's right for *you* – because there are so many systems of monetizing.

How important do you think it is to have a team behind you?

Crucial. Here at my office, we just went through a time where I probably spent the last year and a half going through assistants, being more concerned about cost rather than the quality of people that we need and knowing that it would work out. Again, trusting my heart instead of rationalizing people who are sub-optimal. Really going with my first instinct around, 'who do I know is really good?' and 'would that be value added to my business?' Yes, absolutely, having a good quality team that is well-rounded and a full range of different areas of expertise. What did someone say: find people who love to do what you don't like to do.

So play on their strengths and play on your own strengths?

Absolutely. Be okay with being crappy at doing some things, and find the people that love doing that stuff or who are really good at it. I for one am not very good with the small details, but my assistant, Jeannie, can I tell you, she soars when given the opportunity to organize me and she makes me look great.

At what point were you able to put a team in place with your own business?

Actually it's still happening. We just hired our first sales rep. You wouldn't believe how big my business grew with only two assistants, like a course assistant and a one-on-one client assistant. My business grew *very* big with only two levels of support.

How many do you have now?

Right now, we are four fabulous women and one incredible freedom-seeking man. That's all, my friend! That's on purpose. I'm all about freedom and simplicity. I'm all about the 80/20 rule. This is just me because other people can create bigger teams and they love it. What happened to me when the team started getting too big is that I put everyone else first and not myself. Then I found a team of four people who are all freedom seekers themselves, and all independents, wanting to take care of themselves as well as being really invested in The Vital You and our clients. When I found that team who was committed to the same thing on the planet – a team that wanted to wake people up to ease and flow, and had areas of expertise in the areas that I didn't – look out world, because you've got exponential synchronistic energy flowing! So, yes, I'm very, very blessed. That's what I'm talking about.

Tell me about a typical day for you. Everyone thinks people with money just sit on the beach all day sunning themselves, what do you do?

The great thing is part of my job is to get up in the morning in Bimini, go for a swim with dolphins with a group of people. Come back, do some amazing transformation work, have an extraordinary dinner of lobster we caught that day, have sweet dreams by the ocean, and do it all over again. So when I'm on one of our Soul Adventures, that's a typical day. So, it actually is lying on a beach. That's because that's in the design of what I do, I choose to do life that way. I choose to show other people that it's possible to do that. It's through my example that it's time to be free to live your dreams. So, part of my life is that.

But on a typical day, I get up probably at about seven o'clock in the morning. I have a big smoothie and then I would do some e-mails for about an hour. Then I do my *SOUL E-mail – The School Of Unlimited Life E-wakening* – every morning. Then I probably have about three hours of clients, then lunch. I make about two hours of phone calls to corporate people, to speaking engagements, that kind of stuff, and then probably one or two life or nutritional coaching clients. Then I get out daily for a walk in the enchanted forest for about an hour with my dog, Emerson the wonder dog. I have a few hours of quality time with my special friends and family. I can tell you that we laugh a lot. Then I might have a tele-class or workshops in the evening for parents of freedom-seeking children. I host a radio show throughout the week and am often preparing or conducting interviews with guests and motivational speakers, coaches and interesting people from around the world.

Have you got plans for any more books? You're a best-selling author already, have you got plans to write another in the near future?

Absolutely. The next book is going to be called *Wakey Wakey*. It will be about finding your own personal miracle zone, living on purpose by living in the miracle zone. It's just embodying who you really are and feeling the *wide awakeness* of that. All about saying "yes" to life. Stay tuned, it's on its way and will be published in 2010.

Where did you learn that from, was that from your parents? Were your parents holistic people?

I don't know why I was blessed with this capacity. I think it's partly my dad – I think he's probably a little bit this way. My dad definitely lives by whatever feels best. My mom is a pretty good inspiration, too. But mostly, I spent a lot of time on my own in my teenage years trying to figure out life and following my own barometer. I spent a lot of time feeling out what worked for me, asking lots of questions and I was pretty much of a loner. Then I went out into life and tried to do it society's way, What I figured out and what society's way was, just didn't match up. When I tried to do it society's way, everything felt like a struggle. When I just followed my bliss – like Joseph Campbell says, "follow your bliss" – when I just started following my bliss everything started falling into place and just flowed.

There was still work to do, there were still phone calls to make, and I still had 18-hour days. All that stuff happened. But it was all for the sheer joy of it, rather than working my butt off in order to get somewhere some day. It was for the love of people, for the love of changing their lives, for the love of changing my life and for the love of the testimonials that I get. So it's literally an addictive feeling. I'm excited to get up in the morning and I think the business has just built on itself, evolving ever present and getting better every day.

More information at: www.thevitalyou.com

THREE

Sharon Lechter

Sharon Lechter is an author, entrepreneur, international speaker and educator. She's known worldwide as the co-author of the best-selling book *Rich Dad, Poor Dad*, as well as many other books in the *Rich Dad* series. *Rich Dad, Poor Dad* was originally self-published after having no luck being picked up by a publisher. It has since sold more than 27 million copies and is available in over 50 languages in more than 108 countries. Sharon is the founder of YOUTHpreneur and Pay Your Family First and is currently a member of the President's Advisory Council on Financial Literary.

Q: Sharon, tell us some of your history and how you became involved with financial literacy and how it became a passion of yours.

Certainly. When it comes down to it, people learn about money at home, from their family. That's where I started learning about it. I'm a Certified Public Accountant by training and started my career with Coopers & Lybrand. I think I was the fifth woman ever hired by Coopers & Lybrand in the south eastern United States. From my background in accounting I had the unique opportunity to study businesses that worked and see businesses that didn't work, and learn from the mistakes that other people were making. Then, as I continued through my career, I became very entrepreneurial. I left public accounting and started building my own companies. I met my husband, got married and had three children.

I became concerned the kids didn't like to read so I started working with the inventor of the first talking book – the books with sound strips down the side – and helped him start and build that industry. It was back at the time when bookstores were like libraries, very quiet places. We came on the scene with these talking books, books that made noise. If you fast-forward to today you will see that bookstores now are very interactive and have cafés. We were at the forefront of that back in the late 80's. I was passionate about the talking books because my kids didn't like to read, their friends didn't like to read.

If you jump ahead again to the early 90's, our oldest son, Philip, graduated from high school in 1992. He went off to college in September and by Christmas he had gotten himself into credit card debt, and I was devastated. I had learned about money from my father and I thought I had taught my children about money, taught them the same lessons my father had shared with me. But there was one very big difference, and that was credit cards didn't exist when I was a kid. I was very angry with my son, but most importantly I was angry with myself for not having taught him what he needed. We could easily have bought him out of the problem, but we didn't. It took him five or six years to get himself out of credit card debt, and to get his credit repaired. He still talks about that day and teaches others about the perils of credit cards. He is part of my new company Pay Your Family First, and serves as the president. I'm very proud of him and what he's achieved.

The bottom line is: at that point in time I really defined what I was passionate about. I could combine my passion as a mother with my professional experience both as a CPA and my publishing experience. So my true involvement really started in 1992.

Then in 1996, I was introduced by my husband to Robert Kiyosaki. He had a board game that he had created that was drawn out on a piece of paper, and I saw the value in it. He wanted to write a book and asked me to co-author *Rich Dad, Poor Dad* with him. We released *Rich Dad, Poor Dad* in 1997. We had an incredible 10-year ride of writing books, creating games and were really just blessed with success. But it was not because of us. It was because it was a much- needed message – financial literacy – and the right message at the right time. People found value in it, and it truly was a textbook case of viral marketing. Someone found value and shared it with their friends or family. Every time I meet someone who has read *Rich Dad, Poor Dad* I always ask them: "How did you hear about it?" Invariably the answer is, "My mom gave it to me" or "my friend gave it to me" or "I heard about it at my golf course." It was always something that was referred to them. It was an incredible opportunity to serve others.

Then in January of 2007, 10 years later, Philip blessed me with a grandson. It made me re-evaluate what I was spending my time doing. We were building this big international corporation and our focus had changed to do more of a franchise style business. I really wanted to get back to where my true purpose and my true passions were, and that is financial education for children and families. That's when I left the management of the Rich Dad Company and started working on my new brand, called YOUTHpreneur, and soon to be followed by Familypreneur.

Tell me a little bit more about your goals for YOUTHpreneur.

YOUTHpreneur is really my passion. It's about teaching children about money, as well as families. It's about igniting that entrepreneurial spirit in our young people, getting them to be excited and to learn about finances through experiential learning. There's a lot of content and a lot of curriculum out there that we can just throw on to our kids. But the issue is if they're not experiencing it, they're not learning from it. You don't learn to ride a bike by reading a book. You learn to ride the bike by getting on the bike. You don't learn to snow ski by watching movies. So we want to teach children about money: how you make it; how you keep it; how you invest it; how you save it; and how you benefit your future by becoming financially independent.

Are children interested in money? When you speak to children, what sort of response do you get?

I think it's the thing that they're probably *most* interested in. I always hear people say, "We don't want our kids to turn out greedy. We don't want to teach them about money at a young age." My response to that statement is typically always the same: "At what age do you think a child knows the difference between $1 bill and $20 bill – or a £1 and a £20?" Invariably, by the age of four they know which one is worth more. You offer them a $1 bill and a $20 bill, they're not going to take the $1 bill! They know the difference. They know that one of them has more value. They are bombarded their entire life by marketing messages of how to spend money. As parents, they're with us when we just throw out our plastic and charge things. So they say: "Just charge it Mom." But they're not typically with us when we're paying those bills. They're not with us when we're earning that money. We really need to start showing our children and letting them experience both sides of that economic situation, so they have a better view of the economic world.

What can we do as parents to encourage our children to be entrepreneurs?

Let me start by saying that the best way to do that is to just start talking to them about it. Money is a taboo subject. If there's any benefit from our current economic problems, it is that people are now talking about the economy and talking about the need for financial literacy. Talk to your children about the economic world around you. You can check my website, SharonLechter.com or YOUTHpreneur.com for more information. I have a lot of materials that are free about how to start talking to your kids about money. Just take them to a McDonald's or to a local store and walk them through, and talk about the fact that the wrapper around the hamburger is made by a company. "Is the owner of this McDonald's on the premises? Probably not. That owner has people that they pay to run the restaurant for them. They have another company that provides the cleaning service." Make them aware of what makes the economic world go round and how all these different pieces of the puzzle work together to create a successful business. Just by talking about it, your children will become more aware and interested in it. Think of it in terms of math education in school these days. Today, I can tell you, I've never once used my calculus. We teach our kids Algebra as a math principle, but what if we taught them Algebra using money principles. They might actually relate how it could be used in a practical way and be more encouraged to learn.

The programmes that we've developed at YOUTHpreneur are all experiential learning. We've created it as a way for a young person to start a business, so that they're learning about money when they're actually making it. As a comparison: if you're teaching a class and you're there just dictating to them, telling them "you should save money," it's really a hard task to understand. But compare that task to going into a classroom and showing them, and actually helping them earn money. At the front, say: "If you earn $100, would you agree to put $10 away for charity, $10 away for investing, $10 away for your savings account, and then you could spend the other 70%?" Invariably they say, "yes," because that means they're going to have $70 that they don't have today. It expands their horizons and it gives them the opportunity to become entrepreneurial. It gets them excited about making more. Then the saving and investing and giving back is a benefit to them.

So in other words, make it fun, make it relevant and make sure it's something that they *do* rather than it's a theoretical thing.

Absolutely – and practical.

It's something you think that children even as young as four can get to grips with, even if it's toy money.

Without a doubt. It's a bit too much to start teaching specific lessons at that age, but general concepts are well within a four-year-old's understanding. We have a mentoring package so that you could do it with children as young as eight. The package is geared so that you can do it as teenagers, and even young adults utilise the information. It's geared to be able to be adjusted and used at any age level. The biggest thing is to just *do* it. Our YOUTHpreneur package is for *any* kind of business for a young person – that helps them understand the difference between an active business (where you're selling something to someone else) versus a service business (where you're actually selling your personal services) versus a passive business (which is where potentially, you have an internet business or you have a gumball machine). So we teach the different elements of business to them. But you can take the next step as well and teach this process – it's like a science project – over a six-week time period.

We have it laid out so that through the simple use of a gumball machine, you can teach your child some very important elements – the concept of assets versus liabilities. Of course your machine sitting there is your biggest asset, and the child learns that they can actually make money while they're sleeping as a business owner because they have this asset out there working for them. We've done it in group sets – where a team of three kids will take one gumball machine to one location and another team will take it somewhere else. It's the same machine in similar types of environments, but after a week one machine may have earned $50 and the other one may have only earned $10. It gives us a teachable moment. It's an opportunity for those kids to say: "Well, why did mine make more than yours?" And then they say: "This machine that made $50 was at the front door by customer service. The machine that only made $5 or $10 was back by the bathroom." It gives them an opportunity to understand the importance of location; the importance of signage; the importance of customer service, because one machine might have been cleaner than the other one.

All of these elements are not just important individual lessons, they're life lessons about the importance of your own personal presentation styles. As part of this programme, we teach kids how to make presentations, how to approach the business owners. We have an acronym that we teach. It's B.E.F.A.B. as in 'be fabulous.' It stands for Back Straight, Eye Contact, Firm Handshake, Ask Questions and Allow for Answers, and Be Bold. It's so much fun practising that. What you see is their self-esteem go up, their self-confidence go up. When they realise that they have a tool, that they can help take care of themselves, it empowers them.

You believe that today's economy is the perfect time to start the next Microsoft or the next FedEx, don't you? A lot of people might be surprised to hear you say that with all the bad news that's in the newspapers. Can you explain why you're so upbeat about the economy right now?

Certainly. If you think about many of today's fabulous companies, they were started at times when the markets were at low points. You've got the Googles and the Microsofts – you can go back and figure out when they started and look at the economy. But you can also look at the Great Depression. During the Great Depression many, many of today's successful companies were born. I'm very proud to be associated now with the Napoleon Hill Foundation. The book *Think and Grow Rich* came out during the Great Depression. People had to take care of themselves, and it made them become more creative, it helped them start businesses. It helped ignite the opportunity for people to become entrepreneurs, start their own businesses, and many of those businesses are still successful today. Today we are again in a depressed economy. People are losing their jobs, and people are looking for ways to make money. They'll get creative. It's like a pressure cooker, you'll think about what you can do to make money. By triggering that creativity, people will start businesses today. The market is low, so that people who get in the market over time, they will benefit. Because we talk about how we want to buy low and sell high.

What happens is that people get emotional. What we've seen in the market in the last couple of years, is we've moved from fundamentals to fear. Right now there's no way to justify what's happening in the market, it is very fear based. So we want to help move people from fear to focus, let them start focusing on the fundamentals. For instance, I'm very excited that I have a new book coming out with the Napoleon Hill Foundation and it's called *Three Feet From Gold*. It's all about giving that same message of hope and perseverance. It's the people who continue focusing on their goals, continue working toward their goals with passion and taking the right action, and who are not giving up, that will create those successful companies of tomorrow. The book *Three Feet From Gold* is about turning your obstacles into opportunities.

Great title, I love the title. You're perhaps best known as the co-author of *Rich Dad Poor Dad* – if I can take you back to the time when you first wrote the book, it wasn't all plain sailing was it when you first started out? It's a message that will again give hope to other entrepreneurs or authors.

Absolutely. I remember when we first wrote it, it was actually written as a brochure for the board game. We never expected the book would take on a life of its own. We couldn't find a publisher to publish the book because it was only one title. So my husband and I owned a company called TechPress, and it was actually the original publisher of *Rich Dad Poor Dad*. We just started doing radio interviews all over the country all the time promoting it. We'd be shipping it out from my dining room table. I'd ship the book out to bookstores all over the world because we couldn't get a distributor, or our own shelf space in the stores. In fact, I had a nationwide order from Barnes & Noble and Borders before I ever could find a distributor to even distribute the book for us.

So it was again about keeping focused: continue promoting, continue working, continue marketing, until the right people found it. They found value in it and then they shared it with others.

During the 10 years that you were with the Rich Dad Company – obviously you're no longer there now – it grew into an international powerhouse with over 20 books and board games as well as audio products that you worked on. What are the main reasons that the Rich Dad brand has been so successful compared to other companies?

Our philosophy at Rich Dad was not to be dictatorial, not to preach, but to share these stories and examples. To keep the message simple so that people could understand and could relate to it and could apply it easily to their own life. But I think again it was from people really finding the right message at the right time, people being able to understand it, to relate to it and to easily apply it in their own lives. The simple messages in *Rich Dad Poor Dad* we told through boxes and pictures – easy examples as told through the eyes of a nine-year-old child. It's something that's not at all intimidating. We shared, we didn't tell.

Robert Kiyosaki once said of you, "Sharon is one of the few natural

entrepreneurs that I've ever met. In the Rich Dad Company, I am the horn but Sharon is the engine." Would you say you were a born entrepreneur or was there a learning curve?

It's a combination of the two really. I grew up in an environment, in a home, where my father was a lifelong member of the Navy. He retired, we moved to Florida and he went to work at the Martin Marietta Company and had a whole new career there. But during that time period, he also had real estate that he involved me in. He also had a used car lot that he owned and my mother started her own beauty shop. We had orange groves that we owned. I grew up in an environment where entrepreneurship and owning your own businesses was just part of my life. So when I actually graduated from college and went to work for Coopers & Lybrand, it was like something was missing because I was working for a pay cheque. It was just three or four years after I got out of college, that I felt restless and I wanted to get into more of an entrepreneurial role.

So I do believe entrepreneurship can be learned. But I also think there's a very big piece of it that's innate and that there are certain people that have that thirst for learning. They like to solve problems and they like to be their own boss. But I think there are also people that are very happy just not wanting to pave new grounds, and I think there's nothing wrong with loving being an employee. When I talk about entrepreneurship, I also talk about your personal business. That is: it's not what you do for your pay cheque. When you're working for your pay cheque, it's your job to make money for your employer, that's what you're paid to do. But when you get your pay cheque, what you do with that money is your personal business. It's your personal balance sheet, your personal financial statement. That's why we try to get people to redirect their thoughts. That entrepreneurship can also be 'an entrepreneur of your own wallet' – understanding how you're spending your money and how you are taking care of your family.

One of your aims is to make money work for you, rather than you working for money. Do you believe it's possible for anyone to achieve financial freedom regardless of their background or education?

Yes I do. Obviously education is exceptionally important. Most studies show that the more education you have, typically the higher income you will have. There are only so many CEO positions. I want to bring financial education to anyone who wants it, who seeks it. You don't have to go to college. There are many people who don't make it through high school. They need to have this information available to them. So yes, I definitely encourage college. I encourage post secondary and high school. Definitely the more education you have, the better.

But if you have not had that opportunity, you still have the ability to become financially successful. Understanding assets versus liabilities; understanding to build your personal wealth to the point where you have assets working for you – so you're not the only asset in your balance sheet. Many people today get themselves into so much debt that they can never climb out of it, and that applies to many very highly educated people as well as people who did not have the benefit of education. The problem is we've not taught people about money at any level of education. As a member of the President's Advisory Council on Financial Literacy, we're working very hard to get that financial education at the lower grades K-12 and post secondary, as well as the higher levels.

What sort of message would you give to someone who perhaps has invested in property or stocks in the last couple of years, and they're wondering if they've done the right thing?

First I would say: you cannot change the past, you can only analyse the past. Look and say: "Did I do the right due diligence? Did I buy a stock because I heard my brother-in-law talk about it or did I buy that stock because I researched it and read it?" Everybody makes mistakes. The important thing is you need to learn from those mistakes.

What's happened in the last couple of years in real estate, many of the people that are upside down in real estate are upside down for one of two reasons. One, they expected the value of the real estate to always go up so they overleveraged, and they got themselves upside down with high debts. The second is that they were looking at the real estate as something they could buy and then flip, so they didn't think about cash flow. Real estate investing is a great opportunity today, but we don't know if it's at the bottom. Many say "yes", others say it's not – but it's pretty close to the bottom. Pretty much everybody would agree that over time real estate is going to go up and there will be a huge correction in valuation.

So if you have the opportunity to look at a piece of real estate, look at the cash flow. For instance, I own let's say 10 to 12 properties and all of my properties are cash flow positive which means I receive rent from my tenant that is higher than what I have to pay out each month for maintenance, for taxes and for my mortgage. So the fact that the value of that property drops definitely impacts me, when I look at my net worth. But it will only impact me if I sell that property. I'm still getting a positive cash flow from those properties each and every month. So if you use the fundamentals and you invest in real estate given a cash flow analysis, that's still a great benefit today. If you can find those properties that have tenants, and you can rest assured it will continue to have tenants, you may have the ability to invest in them appropriately with the right fundamentals.

People look at what they did in the market. Yes, no one who has money in the market is happy today, compared to where they were two years ago. But it's a great opportunity to start looking at it, and say, "How can I impact what I'm doing and how can I make sure I have money in an emergency fund?" We talk about diversification. Any financial planner talks about: diversify in paper assets. That's not really diversification. If they look at diversifying in real estate, in owning business *and* paper assets, that's true diversification across assets.

So diversification across assets is what you would recommend?

Yes. Then of course there are also hard commodity assets like gold, silver. You want to make sure you have a *balance* in diversification in all of those categories, real estate, paper, businesses and commodities.

Many entrepreneurs get very overwhelmed when they start out and there are obviously only so many hours in the day to put in the hours. If they had to put in their energies into one thing and one thing only, what would it be?

Obviously, your energy has to be focused on your business and growing your business. When you're an entrepreneur, you need to be your best sales person and you need to be focused on the desired outcome and find people that compliment your talent. The one biggest reason for failure as it relates to lack of capital is this; when you start a new idea you think, 'It's going to be so successful, it's going to take off. It's going to be huge. I only need X dollars to get started.' Almost every time it's going to cost a lot more money than people think because it takes time. You have to develop it. There are unforeseen expenses. So the one thing to focus on is to plan and to take action on realising your dreams, and get more capital than you think you will need.

Do you have any tips for creating a successful brand?

The first tip is to understand that everything you do needs to be focused on your brand. The way to support viral marketing is to make it easy for people to be able to find you. So, it's your look and feel. Your colours should be consistent. Your overall graphic look, which is called trade dress, should be consistent. Your trademark should be things that people can remember and can easily find. You can create sound bytes.

For me it's: 'igniting the entrepreneurs of tomorrow, today'. It's important that your branding is not only a consistent brand, but a consistent voice.

So, drawing on your own personal life as well. It's often said that customers are one of your best forms of marketing, would you agree with that?

They are the *only* important form. I always ask people when I'm doing consulting on businesses: "Are you *selling* your customers or are you *serving* your customers?" If you are *selling*, that's a transaction; you may sell them something once. If you are *servicing* your customers or if you are providing something that they want, something that helps them with their life, something that helps them improve their life, they will come back for more and you will have a relationship with that customer. So you have to say in my business, if I want my business to have longevity, it needs to be a business based on relationships, not based on transactions. In a relationship, that customer will come back to you repeatedly. They will tell others about the service and how they have improved their life with you or your service or your products.

Do you have any rituals that you do every day? For example do you use any affirmations or visualisation or anything like that?

Since early in my career I have a motto. It's two words with a question mark: "Why not?" I think from an entrepreneurial perspective, it's very important. If I'm looking at doing something, I ask myself "why not?" If I can't come up with a legitimate reason why not to do something, I should try it to expand my horizons. It really is my mantra on how I have lived my life: why not try it, why not go for it? Then, the other side of it is that every day I say the prayer of Jabez. It's a little prayer, my rendition is not word for word, you can look it up and get the word for word rendition. It's like: "Dear God, please bless 'lease expand my territory. May your hand be with me.

Please keep me from harm, that I may not cause pain." It's about asking to be of service to others and asking God to assist you in being of service. About being a bigger person making a bigger positive impact on others' lives.

That's very powerful. Your true passion as you've mentioned before is financial literacy for women, for children, for families. Based on your own experience, would you say women face different challenges towards money, towards business, than men do?

Absolutely. The reason behind that I think is just evolution in the traditional family role, and that is women tend to abdicate the financial responsibilities to their husbands. None of us learn about it in school typically, and historically men have been the ones to handle it. So you learn by doing. Women's fear towards money is exacerbated because they've never had to have that experience. I know that I have a dear friend who lost her husband five years ago, and I lost my dad three years ago. Both my friend and my mother were successful professional women. When they got married, they gave that up. They gave up making money, they chose to stay home. My mother then went back and started her own beauty shop, my father always handled the money. My friend married a successful doctor. So they both stopped dealing with money. My mother and father were married 56 years. My friend was married for 25 years. When they lost their husbands, they were very fearful because they hadn't been dealing with money so they felt like they had to learn everything all over again.

I really encourage women to take part in their finances. Women outlive men, women typically end up the sole provider for their own financial life and they've not learned these lessons. So I encourage women to start small and start experiencing and start learning. Women have a lot of fear but they truly know a lot more about finances than they think, they just don't acknowledge themselves. If they've run a charity event for their church, if they've done a fundraiser for their child's school, they've actually been an entrepreneur because all those elements take place. So they've actually started and run a business.

Of course the other aspect is if you educate women, they educate their children.

Right. Through my YOUTHpreneur projects I'm hoping that by having adults, mentors, parents and grandparents educating their children and grandchildren, they'll actually learn a few things themselves.

You've got three children of your own, grown up now. How have you managed to combine your family and your work life over the years?

I love that question because it's one of my bugaboos. I read articles and books, and hear women talk about maintaining balance in their life. It actually irritates me. I can't stand the word 'balance.' We all make choices and we have to make choices that we can live with. When I'm working, I'd rather be with my kids. When I'm with my kids, I know I should be working. So you have to make choices and you have to feel good about the choices that you've made. You can become a better mother if you're successful in business. If you're successful in business and you're taking time to take care of your kids, it will all support one another. So, make the right choices. Think about what you're doing in your day that's not adding value to your children or to your business. Bring in somebody to do your laundry, bring in somebody to do the shopping for you. Don't take away that time where you're reading to your children, don't take away that time where you're having a family dinner, don't sacrifice that.

Look at how you spend your time and see what you can let go of. People talk about having 'to do' lists. Make a 'don't do' list. What can I stop doing and it's not going to hurt me in my relationship with my family or my relationship with my business?

I love that, make a 'don't do' list. That sounds like a really good idea. Tell me a little bit more about being on the President's Advisory Council on Financial Literacy. What sort of recommendations have you been making?

It was a huge honour. It's a tremendous acknowledgement and I'm just very humbled. In January of 2008, President Bush created for the first time the President's Advisory Council on Financial Literacy. Of course given what's happening in the world economy today it's very badly needed. There are 16 of us. Charles Schwab is the chairman, John Hope Bryant is the vice chairman and I'm one of the 14 other members. Now we serve under President Obama. Our commission is for a two-year term through 2010. We are all volunteers, so we're not using taxpayers' money. Our goal is to assess the status of financial literacy in America today and what we can do to increase financial literacy and financial awareness.

We generated a report after a year of study and we have 15 specific recommendations, you can go to the US Treasury Department website to get those. The number one recommendation is that there should be financial literacy required in K-12 and post secondary education. I'm happy to say that since we've actually issued that report, there are now legislative bills on both the House floor and the Senate that would mandate and require K-12 and post secondary financial education. Many states are thinking about it, only a few have mandated specific personal finance classes. But if we can get this through the Federal Government, each state will be required to mandate that there is financial education for every child in America, K-12 and post secondary.

It would be great if other countries around the world would emulate you.

Yes. Many actually are ahead of us. Australia has had this for several years, there are other countries that already require it. It does not matter what country you live in or what language you speak. I've been over the world, and parents all over the world are just as concerned about their children understanding money. There is a need for financial education no matter what your currency is, no matter what language you speak, no matter where you live. Even if you're bartering with a property, we all need to understand the basic economic structure of giving versus receiving, of making money and keeping more than you spend.

You're a great believer in *giving* and that comes across very strongly. You've been given various awards for philanthropy, haven't you?

I have been honoured by several awards, yes.

You're being very modest about the awards. Tell me about the sort of works you have done helping other people…

I'm very honoured to serve on the National Board of the Women Presidents' Organisation. It's an international organisation – a group of women all over the world who own and have built their own businesses. I'm also on the National Board for Childhelp, which is an organisation formed to fight child abuse, and in fact we are celebrating our 50th year in 2009.

I believe that we have a responsibility to support and help others. I definitely believe that you need to teach someone how to fish, not give them fish; you need to teach them how to make money, not give them money.

I don't think of myself as being a giver, I think of myself as being a human being. I was raised with the concept that you are only as good as the people that you help and serve. My dad, when he tucked me in bed every night, would ask me: "Have you added value to someone's life today?"

More information at: www.sharonlechter.com

FOUR

Ali Brown

Ali Brown is the driving force behind a business empire that includes *Ali Magazine,* Ali Boutique and Millionaire Protégé Club.

Her family and friends thought she was crazy when she quit her job at an ad agency in 1998. Shortly afterwards, she set up a small e-zine to help stay in touch with clients. She now has 36,000 subscribers on her mailing list and her company is bringing in seven figures. This was mostly achieved without hiring any employees.

Q: You first set up your business in 1999 without a mentor or a role model, tell me a little about that.

I'd hopped around from job to job in my twenties thinking there was something wrong with me because I would get so restless in normal jobs. All my friends and my parents' friends' kids, they all just seemed fine with jobs and I was so restless. I would want to make changes, I didn't want to work nine-to-five. I knew I was pretty smart, but didn't know really how to change my life. It came to a final straw in about 1999 when I was working at a small ad agency. It was a very small company – there were like seven people in this little office. I liked it because it felt like I was running the place, and I kind of was because these guys running this agency didn't really know what they were doing. I was the one who was doing everything – from working with clients, to fixing the fax machine, to answering phones. Finally, I started thinking, 'Gosh, it seems like I'm running this business – why don't I do this for myself?'

I got to the point that I was just so frustrated one day with some things that were going on that I quit. I had no idea what I was going to do, but it was more painful to stay where I was than to take a complete risk and step out. When I did step out, I was very lost because I didn't have a mentor or a coach. At that time, I didn't know there was such a thing as a mentor or a coach. But the best thing I did was start learning in ways that I could afford. So I started buying books and going to some classes, taking a workshop here or there as I could. That is how I started my very first business, which was copywriting.

I didn't know how to get clients right away, but what I did know a little bit about was e-mail. So I started this small e-mail newsletter with a list of ten people, which included my parents and my cat! From there, I used that little e-mail newsletter to start getting clients. I go into a lot more detail in my programmes on the process obviously, but fast-forward to today I have 36,000 members in my list in a multi-million dollar company. It all started with that day I decided to leave my job and it's been an amazing journey from there.

How did you feel when you first handed in your notice?

I felt a mixture of extreme joy, and there was also some guilt. I was thinking, 'this is really silly, who would give up a job like this, a steady job with decent pay?' But the joy was over-riding. I was excited because I thought, 'at least now that I'm on my own, I'm responsible for my results. If I fail, I'll fail fabulously. But it's my responsibility now. I can figure this out, though I'm not sure how,' but I had the determination to figure it out quickly.

How did you learn about things like money management and building a client database? Was it all a trial and error?

It was all trial and error. I knew nothing. The only resources I had at the time were other people I'd met at these networking groups. After a few meetings, you figured out that they weren't doing too well and they didn't know what they were doing either – we were all pretending. When I started with that little e-mail newsletter, that's when I saw the power of that. People started to forward those e-mails around and people started coming to me to be clients. That's when I saw the power of the Internet. I loved internet marketing, I fell in love with it because it was low cost. It had a broad reach, I mean I can reach people around the world now. It was easy to use, it was easy to do from home. That's when I started just buying everything I could afford – books, e-books, courses on internet marketing – and started studying it.

The day my life really changed is my first day I ever had passive income, and that's when I created my very first e-book. It was called *Boost Business With Your Own E-zine*. I remember going to the gym being very nervous when I pressed 'send' to my e-mail list to launch this e-book. I went to the gym and came back and I had orders in my e-mail box. I was thinking, 'Oh my gosh, I'm not working right now but there's money coming in. I like this. I work a little bit and then I get paid, paid, paid.' That's when I started to learn about leverage, and that is really what changed my business.

You asked about money management – that came later because I had no money at the time. I was putting everything on credit cards and just scraping by. My friends and family thought I was crazy. I bet almost everyone you interview in this book went through the same thing. In the United States I heard a statistic recently from the IRS that less than 6% of the country has an income of over six figures a year. When I first heard that statistic several years ago, a similar statistic, I realized that I had to do the opposite of what most people were doing every day. That was very enlightening because we look around ourselves and see the world operating a certain way, we see people in jobs operating a certain way, we see our family and friends operating a certain way. That was me turning around and completely swimming up-stream. I could only do it because I was so clear in that I didn't want an ordinary life. I was tired of suffering. I wanted to create an extraordinary life. An extraordinary life: a big part of that is an extraordinary income. We're spiritual beings in a very material world, we need to pay the mortgage and we need to take care of ourselves. I made it a priority to start learning how to make money.

Why do you think you've been so successful when so many other people fail?

For me I believe it's that I have absolute persistence and focus. I was probably willing to make sacrifices that some people wouldn't have. Those first few years were very hard. There were many times that I came close to giving up or throwing in the towel. But I knew deep down not only that I wanted to be successful, but I knew I had a bigger purpose in the world. I believe that's true for all of us on this planet. You were here for a reason and it's not just to go to a job from nine-to-five. You're here to create an amazing life for yourself. For some of us, we want to create an amazing life for other people as well. I did always like helping people and I saw the direct connection between my being successful and then being able to help other women become successful. I noticed each level that I'd step up and get a little further, I had more people asking me questions: "How did you do this? How did you get clients? Can you come talk to us on how you do e-mail marketing?" I would just love to share.

Then I learned a bit more and did a bit more and got more successful, and then people would want me to share that. Tapping into the *giving* as well as the doing is what really fuelled me and kept me going those few years when things were very hard. I think when people give up, when they give up on their dreams, it's because of a lack of confidence. I'll tell you though, I never saw all the answers there – but I had faith. Faith is a huge component of being a successful entrepreneur because there are many times you do not see what's on the other side of the door. You can feel it, you're close to it, you can almost taste it. You can taste that success, but your fear is like a combination lock. If you don't move through your fears or have the courage to step through from making some changes in your life – and some of them are scary – you won't ever see what's on the other side of that door.

One of your missions is to help women 'create their own economy.' Can you explain what you mean by that?

Most people are making decisions based on the economy. They're watching way too much news, they're listening to the talk at the coffee shop or around them – people complaining and saying things are so bad, when what they should be focusing on is creating their own economy. Actually at the time that you're interviewing right now, we're in a financial credit crunch here in the United States as well as many places around the world. There has never been a more important time for women to step up and take control of their income. Actually we're seeing more sign-ups for our programme than we ever have before. Our business will probably double again this year for our coaching and our entrepreneurial programmes. We think it's because women are getting the message sooner than the men are. They're feeling – this big shift in the world right now – that things are changing and the old way of doing things isn't going to work any more.

I love men and we all need masculine energy in the world. We need masculine energy in our business otherwise we'd never get anything done, we'd be lounging around all day and braiding each others' hair! But that feminine energy though is starting to come back into balance. That's what you're feeling right now, this balance in the world. It's a new way of doing things – a way of doing things with grace and ease, helping each other and helping communities at the same time. There are a lot of people who go into business or start a mission because they want to change *the* world. But what I emphasise in my programmes is that you have to start with *your* world. By changing *your* world, that will change *the* world – but you can't change *the* world until you start changing *your* world. You can't help women in Africa, around the world, in a true powerful way until you can pay your own mortgage and take care of your family. So, start there and give what you can. But you have to build success for yourself before you can truly give in a global powerful way.

You describe internet marketing as a 'recession-proof' business. Can you tell me why it's so recession-proof.

It's wonderful because nowhere else is there a way of creating products and programmes that people need. There's all kinds of ways to do research in what people are searching for, what they're looking for. What I teach – information marketing – is a way to do this that you can create products and programmes that people are already looking for. One of them – the core part of my 'online success blueprint' that I teach – is building a list of prospects for your business. What this will do for you, which many people overlook, is actually give you an audience to market to for years to come. What most people do when they start an internet business is they think of a product and then start with the product idea. What they should do, which is contradictory to what everybody thinks, is they should actually first look at *who* they want to market to.

As an example, there's a client of mine named Ciara Daykin, she's a wedding planner. But now she's creating a coaching programme for other wedding planners, because Ciara was really doing well as a wedding planner and having a six-figure business. Now she's turned it around, she wants to share with other wedding planners how they can have successful businesses as well. Because she knows her market – wedding planners – she can continually create products or programmes that will help them and that they want and need.

What would you say is the biggest roadblock to success? What's the thing that's stopping most people?

It's actually getting out of their own way. When people talk about reasons they can't do something, these are usually almost always self-created limitations. I hear people complain for example, "I can't do that because I have a family" or I can't do that because I'm a single mom" or "I can't do that because I live here or there" or "I can't do that because I'm overweight" or "I don't know what to do." Every excuse people can come up with, I can show them a success story of someone who has done it. It's really about making the decision to be successful, and many people haven't done that. A lot of us don't learn how to do this growing up. Actually the Latin root of the word 'decide' means to cut off. You're cutting off all other options. You're saying to yourself, "This is it, I'm doing this. Come hell or high water, I'm going to be successful." When you have that "whatever it takes" attitude, that is what takes people to a completely different level.

I have women in my programmes who are single moms and just working part-time, but they're still having successful businesses. I have people in my programmes who have come from dire circumstances and turned their lives around. It's very, very inspiring, and it really comes down to just having the willpower and saying: "I deserve this and I'm going to do whatever it takes to change my life."

Where did you get your self-belief and willpower from? Did you have very supportive parents – did you have an entrepreneurial family?

That's a good question. I am very lucky that my parents were still together until my father passed away last year and I had a good childhood. Although I'll tell you, my mom was such a worrywart, she was a big worrier. Even today, she has that negative attitude about things like, "I hope something doesn't happen" or "I hope that this or that doesn't go wrong" and that's just how she thinks. So I grew up with that, that was challenging and it took a lot of undoing. I was kind of a late bloomer. I did okay in school but it wasn't until I got into the working world, and even better *out* of the working world, that I started seeing the correlation between setting my mind to something and getting it done. It is about setting the intention and just claiming that it is done. It starts with law of attraction, but law of attraction wasn't meant to be an end, it's really the beginning. That starts the process and then you have to take action from there.

In many businesses, people are spending 20% of time doing 80% of the money-making. What would you say is the single most important area that you're spending time on?

When you start a business, you're doing everything. You're writing the e-mails and you're creating the bold new ideas and you're going to the post office and you're doing everything. As you move up and are able to hire help, this is the best thing you can do as you grow a business. I always encourage my students to hire an assistant as soon as they can and often before they think they need it. What you just brought up – the 80/20 rule or Pareto principle – is a crucial thing to understand in running a business. When you want to be a visionary, when you want to be an entrepreneur, a true CEO, the idea generator and the money-maker, all you should be spending your time on is the brilliant work. So, creating bold new income streams or working with your clients for a high fee.

Now when you're starting a business, that's not possible all the time because you're still answering the phone and doing all those other things. But little by little, you should wean out the things that aren't making you the money right away – either delegate it, delete it or automate it. There are ways to do all three. For me personally, right now I spend almost all my time creating bold new products and programmes to help the women in my group. That is why we've been so successful. That's one of the big reasons is that I've been able to focus on that now by leveraging a team.

How important do you think it is to have that team and how do you choose your team members?

I made it to seven figures without having any employees. It is absolutely do-able. I had two virtual assistants. I actually made seven figures by learning how to leverage my programmes, and introducing higher priced programmes and services for the people who wanted more help from me. I noticed though when I hit seven figures, my poor team would start saying things like, "We can't get this done on time" and that's when I knew it was time to hire more people. I suggest that people start off with one or two assistants, and you only want to hire as needed. For a long time I didn't want any employees because I tell you, I live here at the beach, I love being in flip flops and I don't want to see anybody. I love working alone and having privacy.

But this past year, I made a very conscious decision that I was going to grow this business to a whole new level. I had to do a little thinking about that because I didn't want to give up that lifestyle I'd created of being here at the beach and setting my own schedule, being able to wear my sweats and flip flops, have my hair in a ponytail and go for walks on the beach. I don't want to go work in an office and have this corporation. But I saw the opportunity this year to take this business to a whole new level so that I could help women around the world. So I made that decision. We do have an office now and I do have employees. But guess what? I'm not there. I'm sitting here right now talking to you from my couch at the beach house. So I'd vowed as I was doing this, and building the business, it would still be designed around the life that I wanted.

I think that's very important for any business owner to know, especially women. We often create things without taking our own needs into account. Ladies, think about the life that you want to design, and then use your business to help design that life. So, you don't want to see people in the house? That's great, you can use virtual assistants. If you need an office, go into the office two days a week, but other people can be there full-time. There's many ways of designing your business around what your needs and values are.

What tips would you give someone who wanted to start out tomorrow? If they have to do something for the next three days or the next week, what would your top tips be?

If they have an existing business, I'd look at two things. Number one, what are your natural gifts and talents? What is your 'magic', we call it. Many of us overlook our own magic. We take it for granted that we may be good at some things or have a knack for talking to people about something or coaching them through something. This may be something you need to ask your colleagues or clients or friends and family about, like "what do you think are my natural gifts that I'm good at?" The second thing I would say is: what type of audience do you want for your products and services and what are they looking for?

For example, let's say you are a mom who's been home-based and you're ready to start a business – I could use a friend as an example. She just lost her job after 15 years at a Fortune 500 company. Fifteen years, can you imagine? She wants to start a business as an image consultant. So the first thing she did is look at her own special gifts and the things she loves. Her name is Stephanie, and all of us around her said, "Stephanie, you dress like you stepped out of a catalogue. I don't think you notice." She's always the gal you call to ask if this top goes with this bottom or what do you think of this necklace or can you help me find a scarf to go with this. This is her natural gift, it's her magic. What I'm having Stephanie look at now is: where's the market?

So, first you look at your gifts and talent, then you look at your market and look at what *they* want right now. Let's say Stephanie may love just dressing people up for the weekends, but people may not want to be paying for that. But people going on job interviews would much more likely pay for image consulting if they think it would help them get the job. Does that make sense? So, looking for ways to take your magic and get it to the market in a way that they would want to jump at the opportunity. So, those are the few things you really need to look at before you start marketing. If you start marketing without knowing those two things, you're really going to have a hard time.

How about you – is there anything you would have done differently over the years?

I love that question. Everything. One thing I did accidentally, which was the best thing I ever did, was start that darn newsletter. I thought that was just a fun little thing. But starting that e-zine – I didn't even call it that at the time, it was just an e-mail newsletter – is what has allowed me to continue to generate income in larger and larger amounts by having that list at the push of a button. I think if I could go back and do anything differently, I would have started that even earlier and started building the list earlier in different ways. That way I'd have even more people on the list and be able to help more people as I go.

Describe a typical day for you. You described being in flips flops and hanging out around the house. How do you start and finish your day?

This morning I had a very good friend stay over with me last night. I have a great guest room with an ocean view, so once they find out about that it's hard to make them leave! We got up this morning, we had a little breakfast and some tea, and then we went for about an hour's walk on the beach – it's gorgeous here. I checked my calendar first, I saw I didn't have any calls until 11 am. So we went for a nice, long walk. I came back, I had an energy shake and then my personal assistant, Amanda, is here at the house. She came today with groceries and fresh flowers, and she helps me keep the house organised.

Buying this house last year was a stretch for me, it's a large home, but I wanted the space to expand. I was going through this big expansion in my life, not only mentally and financially, but I wanted that physical space to grow into. So, Amanda's here three days a week to make sure that I have healthy food in the fridge and to bring fresh flowers. She waits for the cable guy if we need that. It's wonderful to have her here.

So, she was here this morning, I had two coaching calls with members of my diamond tier of the Millionaire Protégé Club. Those are my clients that pay $100,000 to work with me. I love working with them because you can bet they're serious and they move forward quickly – it's such a joy. Then I had a call with my team about one of our programmes we're planning up to launch. Then I'm doing this call with you, and then I'm probably going to take a catnap. I'm a big fan of naps, they really give me a boost late in the day and clear my head. I'll do a little bit more work, and then tonight is massage night. I have a great guy named Fernando that comes to the house on Monday nights. This is a lovely day. If I could design every day to be like this, it would be like this.

Tomorrow is a little heavier; I have a full day of coaching calls from about 10 am to 6 pm with a lunch break in between. So it really varies, it comes in cycles. If we're getting ready to launch a new programme, the whole team is a little busier. If we slow down, then I'm not working every day at all. It's up and down, but I love that it's flexible and I can really plan around my life. I had a good friend here. I did have a call scheduled earlier this morning, I called my team and I said: "Can you move that call because it's really important for me to take a walk on the beach with my friend."

So you find it quite easy to balance home and work life?

I do. Some may say it's because I'm single. That is easier. I do know many single moms who have a harder time of course. That's why you have to get in juggling childcare, making sure you have more time. It's even more important for moms and women with families to get really good at managing their time. So, I teach that as well. Because I am single now and I'm waiting for Mr. Right, I am working a little more. I'm building the castle now. That way I'm doing this now while I have the time and the energy. That way, one day if I do want to have a family that option is there.

How often do you keep in touch with clients in terms of your mailing list or e-zines? How often do you contact them?

I'm in touch with my main list of 36,000 members at the very least once a week. If I had to recommend a schedule, I would say no less than once a week. If we are launching something exciting and we want to make sure they know about it, they can get an e-mail from us every two to three days. It's a fine balance and you'll know when you've crossed the line if you see people unsubscribing, getting ticked off. But generally, you have to watch your sales. Some people are very timid about contacting their clients and prospects. If I just want to send something out once a month, it's not even worth it then. I really want people to contact their clients and prospects at least once a week.

Once a week ideally – and really you should monitor your opt-in rates and your opt-out rates to see how your clients are responding. So, all the time have an eye on your clients?

Yes, you'll know, when you've crossed the line you'll know. You're like, "Okay, I shouldn't have sent out that last e-mail." But you never know until you do. If you're getting more sales and only losing a few people who weren't going to buy from you anyway, that's why you have to watch the big picture.

How do you get your clients to refer their friends to you?

We don't have any formal referral programme. We do have an affiliate programme which is similar. For those people who aren't familiar with online marketing and affiliate programmes, it's where many of our clients will refer my programmes and products to their friends and then they are gifted with a thank you commission if they refer someone who does buy a product or programme from us. So that's a nice way of saying thank you for results. We don't really have an official 'refer a friend' programme, even for the e-mails. It's something we probably should have had in place a while ago. But the affiliate programme is great because people are talking about our stuff all over, especially with the social networking. If you're on Twitter or Facebook, you'll see people promoting my programmes and products. I love it because you get results and you only pay for results. Everyone should have an affiliate programme. It's a wonderful thing that any business can start.

What would you say motivates you at this stage? You've built your business up into a big multi-million dollar business. What is it that drives you and makes you get up every day?

I have to tell you, in the beginning what drove me was paying the rent. In the beginning, the money definitely motivated me. I won't say it doesn't any more – I think money is a wonderful thing and we can use it for wonderful things. Money should be to give us beautiful experiences and beautiful environments. Women love pretty things and we should have pretty things. What's interesting is the last year when I made this conscious decision to take the business to a $50-100 million level; that's what we're visioning right now. That's going to change because I know this is going to take more work than I've done before. Stepping into that is because there's a deeper purpose to it. I have a mission to be helping women around the world start their own businesses and learn about entrepreneurship, because this will give women more power back in the world. It will help correct this balance of the world's energy being off for so long in this masculine way. You can feel the shift starting to happen and I want to be a part of that. I want to help lead that change around the world.

Once you tap into your purpose, that is what drives you more than anything. It's amazing, when you align your purpose with the profits, everything just starts lining up and opportunities are dropping in my lap. Things are clearing out of the way, it's as if the universe is laying a path before me. It's a combination of becoming aware of my purpose and listening to my heart and listening for clues and also getting serious about the business.

You mentioned earlier taking risks – leaving your job and taking what seemed like a risk at that time. How big a risk do you think entrepreneurs should take? Should they take big risks, small risks, or just what their intuition tells them?

I think it's a smart risk, if that makes sense. When I quit my job, I had an idea of what I was going to do. I didn't have a client yet, but I knew I had an idea. I knew I was good at what I did, and I had a feeling that if I just put my nose at the grindstone I could find a client. I think you should have a reasonable sense of confidence in yourself before you take a leap like this. The challenge is that most of us as we're raised in childhood, in school, are taught to take small steps. In school we go to first grade, second grade, third grade. In the corporate world we start as assistants – I started as a receptionist making coffee – and you work your way up to being an account executive, then a manager, and so forth. When you're an entrepreneur you suddenly realise there are no rules, and this freaks a lot of people out because they don't know how to handle it. So they keep taking small steps when actually, it's not harder to make a huge leap in your income and your life than it is to take a small step. You just have to embrace thinking completely differently.

I encourage everyone to make leaps, but you have to know in your heart that you can be confident in yourself. If you don't have the confidence, if you make decisions out of fear, then you will fail. If you make decisions out of complete faith, you just say: "I'm doing this. I don't know the 'how' yet, but I *know* this is going to work. I'm going to make it work. I have complete confidence in myself. I don't know why, but I do." You're talking yourself into it. If I made any decisions based on numbers or my current circumstances, I would still be back in that job right now. I would never have moved forward. I make decisions not from where I *am*, but from where I want to *be*. That has changed my life. Also, when you get very clear in the next leap you want to make, you are then pulled forward instead of having to push up the ladder.

You mentioned gender differences earlier. Do you think that men and women have different challenges when it comes to making money?

I do think that men seem to take risks more easily. I'm sure many people would agree with me – I'm not aware of any studies on this. Women are very timid about making risks, sometimes because we feel that also it may impact on other people in our life and not just us. Also many of us worry maybe about what other people will think. When I've coached some of my clients, I drill down to the big reason why they are not doing something. Sometimes, it will come down to 'what other people think of me'. They realise it's not that they're going to fail, it's that other people will see them fail. When we get around that stuff and just get their head back on straight, that's when you start seeing the magic.

The good news is that decades ago it was very hard for women to be entrepreneurs. These days with all the information technology, the ways we can work from home and also the way that most businesses have become about communication, we are so natural for these types of businesses and starting these businesses from home or wherever we want to start them. We love communicating, we love community, and women are helping women now like never before.

You mentioned plans to grow your business. What are your plans for the next couple of years?

This year we launched the brand new *Ali* magazine. You can also get a subscription overseas. We just launched the first ever women's magazine that combines being an entrepreneur with having a wonderful, fun life. It has articles on female icons like Ivanka Trump and Angelina Jolie, and celebrities who are doing great things in the world and businesswomen doing great things. But we also talk about the latest great shoes and how to look good when you go to meetings and how to balance your family life, things you can be doing with your kids. There's no other magazine like it, and people are flipping out. We are taking that to news stands this year. That was our big leap this year.

As I grow the media empire, that's going to be a platform for launching a global outreach for women around the world and helping them embrace entrepreneurship. The big picture is that the more women in the world who learn how to create incomes for themselves will lead to world peace. That is the big picture. It's so big and so heavy that I don't share it often but I want to share it with you. When you think about it, women own less than 1% of the wealth of the world right now. If more women can learn how to start businesses for themselves, help themselves and their families and their communities, you will see a shift in the world that's about to happen like never before. Everyone is jumping on this bandwagon, they're so excited and you can feel it. The world is pulling together right now. You see in the news all this doom and gloom, it's a lot of BS really. This is one of the most beautiful times in history that we're about to witness and I'm really excited to be a part of it.

Where does your passion come from? When did you realise that was what your purpose was? Was there a defining moment or did it happen in slow increments?

It happened in slow increments. You have friends who kind of smack you on the head and say: "Don't you see this?" This is why everyone needs a coach. I have coaches and mentors myself. My coach said: "You're going to be a leader in the world spotlight." When I first heard her say that I was just chuckling. I'm like: "Come on, I just have this internet business." But now I feel it. Once I got that idea, and just started stepping out bolder and bolder, I'm having more and more success. I'm seeing more women follow, and I'm helping more women. I just want to keep that trend going and it's going to be amazing. I love nothing more than seeing other people's lives influenced. That brings me more joy than anything in the world. I truly am here to leave a legacy. I've only just started tapping into it.

When you were a child, suppose you were eight years old, what did you think you were going to be when you were older?

When I was five, I told my mom I wanted to be either a paediatrician or a backup singer. I have no idea why. I always thought I'd be in the corporate world and have a corner office, but I didn't think I'd be owning the whole company.

At what point did you think you were going to own a company?

I think in my twenties when I started working for other people. I was looking at my bosses and thinking, 'Well, if these nitwits can do it...'

More information at: www.alibrown.com

FIVE

Barbara Corcoran

Barbara Corcoran started a tiny real estate company after quitting her job as a waitress. Over the next 25 years, she turned it into a 5 billion dollar business. Barbara is also a best-selling author and appears as the sole female entrepreneur on the TV show 'Shark Tank'.

Q: Barbara, you got straight D's in high school and college. You had over 20 jobs by the time you turned 23 and you then famously borrowed $1,000 from a boyfriend and your life changed forever. Tell me exactly what happened.

I was working as a waitress and fortunately Ramóne Simóne was his name – Ramóne Simóne with an accent on the O's or whatever he did – ordered a cup of tea at my counter, which was very lucky because he offered me a ride home. I lived one town away, which was about half a mile away from the diner. He drove me home and that was the beginning of our relationship. Ramóne was about 10 years older than me, and from a whole different world – or so he said. He said he had been raised in the Basque Country, as in Spain. He had olive skin, dark sunglasses, jet-black hair. He had a very shiny suit on and I had never seen anything like it.

So he drove me home in his very fancy yellow car, which was a Lincoln Continental, and drove me to my family's house. We had in our family 10 children and I was the second oldest. So that night he walked in and met (I don't think my older sister was home) but he met at least nine out of the 10 kids and they just loved him! They thought he was like a Hollywood rock star walking into our house with the car running outside. It was like we had been *found*, but my parents hated him on sight. I think they saw him for who he was, 10 years older than their young daughter and Trouble!

So he proved to be trouble in their eyes, but he also proved to be the luckiest break I ever got. The trouble he caused was he encouraged me to move to New York City, and in fact he offered to pay for a week at a women's hotel in New York that was quite respectable. You had to wait in the lobby if you were a date, you couldn't go upstairs. I guess he thought that would make my mother happy. She was *not* happy. She'd forbidden me to go, but I went anyway and I never moved back to New Jersey again. One thing led to another after that. Within that year, he loaned me the $1,000 to start the real estate business. Why I started that business? He just said I'd be great at real estate and he seemed to be a man of the world who would know that kind of thing. So I said "okay" and we started a partnership together.

So would you say he was your first mentor?

Definitely. I don't think we even knew the word 'mentor' back then quite honestly. I think that's more of a modern day word, but he was my boyfriend, my man about town, my counsellor. So if that all adds up to a mentor, that's what he was. He was a super mentor because he covered all bases. He was my lover as well.

So that was what gave you the courage to take that first step?

It wasn't even a courage thing. I assumed he knew what he was doing. He sure looked and acted the part and I figured anyone who could come all the way from the Basque Country and have a big car like that had to know what he was doing. I later found out he wasn't from the Basque Country. His mother told me he was from 145th Street, otherwise known as Harlem. I also learned his name wasn't Ramóne Simóne, it was Ray Simon. So he was a great self-marketer – I remember my mother saying after she met him that first night, "He's a phoney" and my outraged response. "How could you say he's a phoney? You're just uncomfortable because you've never met anyone like him," blah, blah, blah. But of course, my mother was right, she always was. But he was a good phoney because he was someone who had come from nothing, with nothing going for himself, and made a success of himself. So he just merchandised himself in a much more interesting way, which was certainly impressionable on a young 23-year-old.

So how did you carry on with the partnership with him and then set up on your own?

Something went awry. He fell in love with my secretary, Tina. Those little details make a change. But what happened is I moved in with him, about a year and a half after I stayed at that hotel. Initially, I got two roommates, and then later I moved in with Ray. But once I moved in, I also found out he had three young daughters and they moved in with us too! So I became Mrs. Mom at a very young age raising those three girls.

So seven years after I had met him, (I was his sort of wife – even though

I wasn't a wife) he came home one night while I was making pasta for the girls. I remember it because I was dumping the pasta in the strainer and the steam was in my face, and he said: "We have something serious to discuss." I said: "What's that?" He said: "I'm going to marry Tina." I couldn't believe it. It seemed like a joke.

Anyway, I moved out that night and then I continued to work with him – and Tina – because he reminded me that I couldn't fire Tina, which I wanted to do because it was very uncomfortable. But he reminded me he was the 51% partner and I was the 49% partner and he was in charge, which was true. He had never used that before, but he clearly was in charge.

So that lasted for about a year and a half and Tina moved into my desk in his office, because we shared an office, and I sat on the outside. I wish I had a good story to tell you about why I decided to end it: I really have no idea why I did it, why it took so long or what came into my head. Just one day I said: "I'm not doing this any more". So I walked in and announced that we were ending the partnership.

The way we did it was just like a football draw in America. He picked the first person – we had 14 salespeople at the time, so we had a tiny but still successful brokerage firm. We had 14 happy salespeople and it was really like breaking up a marriage. They thought of us as Mom and Dad in a way, even though most of the people in that company were older than me by far, but we were the parents and they were the kids. So we divided them into groups of seven. Then I said: "You decide to stay or you could go," and he said, "I'll stay." So he stayed. Then I said: "You can take the phone number or get a new one." He said: "I'll take the old number, you get a new one." So I moved my seven people out at the end of that work-week and that was the beginning of Corcoran Group.

So actually, what seemed like bad luck at the time turned out to be a brilliant move?

Easy to say in hindsight.

Yes, as things always are.

It's always bad when it's bad. It only gets good with time. But thank God for those departures on the road. They make all the difference in life.

So these must have been very difficult and traumatic times?

Do you know why it's so? If you think about it, I always felt that Ramóne (or Ray as I now call him) found me in a little town where no one could find me. He gave me a shot at the big city. He gave me my confidence. He said he thought I would be great at something – nobody had ever said that before – and he thought I was young and beautiful and capable. So everything associated with him to that point was very positive. Because I had come out of a school system where I was a terrible student, and I hadn't really had success in that environment, I felt suddenly successful.

So of course, when that boat pulls out, you wonder if you're going to sink and I was convinced I couldn't float without him. But as it turned out, I found I was pretty adaptable. If you swim hard enough, you not only float but you actually can move faster. I started swimming for my life, as I had never done before. Like most good deeds that you put a lot of energy into, they generally pay off. So the business started getting built little by little, and then the rest was just building mass and productivity and hiring the right people, etc., – things that everybody does when building a business.

You mentioned that no one had ever said you were great before and that you had little success in school. Where did you get your self-belief from?

From my mother. I probably misrepresent myself saying no one had ever. I had a mom who told me almost daily that I was almost a genius. She always said I was creative. She labelled me as creative and she said that I could figure anything out. Even when I had that dreaded day, (in third grade I guess it was) where I was told by the nun-from-hell that I was stupid, my mother's way of handling it that day was to say: "Don't worry about it." She said: "You have a wonderful imagination and you'll learn to fill in all the blanks." So she dismissed it as though as it was totally unimportant. Of course, as a kid in a classroom where kids are judged by school grades and how well you do in that very narrow definition of intelligence, it was a big deal. But in my mother's mind it was just a small point, because she knew I had a great imagination and that was my forté. So I had constant positive reinforcement at home just like I had negative reinforcement in school. So thank God for that, it certainly offset it. So even though I felt like a failure at school, clearly, day in and day out, I felt very successful at home with my siblings and my mother.

Over the next 25 years, you grew that loan of $1,000 into a billion dollar business – and eventually sold it for $70 million...

I actually sold the business for $66 million. I don't know, everybody always says $70 million. I don't know where that came from, but it's actually $66 million because that was my lucky number and that's how I arrived at the sale price. I just gave them my lucky number. They didn't know how I arrived at it. They went crazy with their accountants and attorneys trying to justify it, thinking there was some rhyme or reason, but I was laughing on the inside. But I missed your question.

Yes, basically, how did you manage to do that?

That's a huge question of course, a million details that somehow come together. A lot of mistakes that somehow you get away with. I would say piles of both: good judgements and bad judgements, but a lot of effort. I think that's true of most people who do well in anything, they put in an inordinate amount of effort and I certainly did that. I'd been working seven days a week. I worked since I was 11. I worked after school every day; I worked every summer. But when I was in my own business I was in work at like 7:10am usually at my desk, out showing properties by 9am and I finished up my paperwork probably every night by 11pm. I lived for my work. That's all I did is work.

So that's how you do that mostly, just by breaking your back over it. But I also loved every minute of it and I think that was a magic ingredient. If I had been in the wrong field that didn't suit my personality, long hours would have been terrible. But I was in something that didn't feel like work, it felt like play. For me all it was, was socialising with people. I loved being around people, meeting new people, laughing, being out in the street – not having to be locked behind a desk all day. Not having a boss was a big one that I took for granted, I didn't realise how important that was until I had it. So all those things somehow come together.

Plus I had the very good fortune of being in New York City where it's easier to succeed than anywhere else. I've often sat back and thought, "I would've never had this success if I had been in Cincinnati or Detroit or San Francisco." New York is a real estate town. It's all about money. It's all about business. I had that backdrop that accommodated me and I had it every day. Every day, every working minute I was doing my thing on a stage that valued those things.

Also, the other reason I always felt I did so well was because New York was a town that placed no value on your background or your pedigree. People would say: "Where did you go to school?" They'd never heard of my school because there were only 13 kids in the class, it was a new school. But no one placed a value on that. Maybe if you get a banking job, but certainly not a real estate broker's job. So nobody really cared where I was from. Nobody cared if my parents had money or not. All they cared about is: could I help them now and could I really succeed in making the deal, was I the best person to work with. They loved me to death and referred me to the next client and the next client. So my business really did grow for a new business. It grew very quickly and steadily because I felt like I made a friend of everyone I worked with.

I got off course here. What I was trying to say is the city I worked in very much accommodated me. Then also, I had the good fortune of starting the business at the right time in the early 1970's, before New York prices had gone through the roof and outward to Mars...

I came in at the worst, darkest hour for real estate. I also came in right at the cusp when it was about to change. So that was nothing more than good luck. If I had been there five years earlier, I probably couldn't have made the sales. If I had come into the market five years later, I would have had to compete with that many more firms. The biggest firm I had to compete with when I got started had 32 people. I thought they were a monster – a powerhouse. When I sold my business, I had 1,400 people and I was the largest by far. But by then, the big companies in town had more than 300. So they had multiplied times 10 at least or by 100 in size. So that was very lucky too, if you think about it. All those stars aligned for me, all I had to do was work it.

It must have been an incredibly sharp learning curve in the early days. How did you know about things like picking the right people?

Well, I trusted my instincts and I basically picked people I liked, who had energy. I know that's probably not the right way to hire, but for me it always worked out. If they had high energy, I could see they were going to work hard. If I liked them, I figured I was liking them for some reason, I often didn't question why. I figured if I liked them, the client was going to like them. I didn't care what they knew, but actually in those days no one had real estate experience. People who had larger firms than mine certainly weren't going to come over to my shop, because I wasn't respected and I wasn't large, I didn't have a brand.

But so far as who I interviewed on a day-to-day basis, who I was able to hustle into the firm, none of them knew anything about real estate other than the fact they lived somewhere – they lived in an apartment or a house. But it wasn't important. What was important I found was the people, if they had energy. What came automatically with energy was a positive outlook because people with a negative outlook never have energy from what I can see.

So if they had abundance of energy, they were usually abundantly optimistic. If they were likable, that comes with a whole cluster of things that sometimes you don't know how to articulate. Like if you like someone you usually also trust them, you usually also think they know what they're doing whether they do or don't. I could have a new broker go out on a Monday with a new client never having shown anything. But if they're personable and do it enthusiastically, usually the client wasn't on to them that they'd never shown an apartment before, unless they walked in the wrong direction. In Manhattan, even that was good. We were a perfect grid. As long as you knew that 21st Street came before 22nd Street, you could usually get there.

You were leading a team of over 1,400 brokers at one point. How did you learn to be a good leader? Was that something that you did intuitively or did you have to learn how to do that?

Well you learn pieces of it along the way, no doubt through the mistakes you make. Certainly, I made a few whoppers along the way on people, but not many. Those weren't my real whoppers. My real whoppers were spending money I didn't have that I shouldn't have spent. That's where I usually went awry many times…

Again, I'm not trying to make it too simple, but I think if you're wildly enthusiastic about whatever you're doing, people will follow you because people want some fun. They want to be able to be happy like you. So I think people instinctively follow someone who deserves to be followed. I think the attraction there is this sheer love affair the person is having with what they're doing. Clearly, you have 'bad' days too. They were usually bad financial days when the market went awry, and you didn't know how you were going to stay in business or how you were going to meet your bills. Those are the bad days.

But short of those days, every other day was a blast. You picked up the phone – you had no idea who was going to be on the other end of that line. You met somebody on the street – you had no idea, except for that short phone conversation, how much time you might be spending with them; whether it would be a successful sales call. How long you might be working with them or how short; whether they were phoney, whether they were real; whether they had a real need to move or whether they were just jerking you around. It was always a Pandora's Box in the best way.

Remember, you had all these people coming into New York, in a city that virtually had no native New Yorkers. Everybody was from somewhere else, people who were buying here anyway, they were from somewhere else. So you'd get to meet usually the most successful people in every field from all over the world. Who wouldn't covet a client-base like that? It was never boring. To this day, you talk to any real estate broker in Manhattan, even the unsuccessful ones; you could not get anyone to say they've ever had a boring day. It's just not doable. Too much motion and change in this town for that.

Your passion and your love for your business comes across really strongly. What advice would you give to other entrepreneurs who want to grow their business like you did?

I think a lot of people are working a wheel that they're not having a love affair with, and I don't think you'll ever become successful that way. So I think the key is finding something you really enjoy doing. I know it doesn't sound like solid business advice, but it's a great place to start. What do you really like? A lot of people get hobbies mixed up with occupations – my first husband was one like that. He tried to make a business out of carving ducks. But I think you have to ask yourself: "What do you like to do?" and then can you make a living at it. In other words, does it pay? If not, it's a hobby. But if you could combine those two, something you love to do that actually can pay your bills, I think you're half way there. Then if you just put the work into it, the hours into it, why would you not succeed? I think you have the magic ingredients right there all bundled in one tight little package.

What about branding? Do you think branding – and marketing – is part of the key to success?

It depends what you're after. For my business, branding was why we were so successful without a doubt. If we had great branding but we had lousy people, we would not have succeeded. But if you have a team of good people, even if you have a few clunkers mixed in (which is human nature, you can't spot everybody). But let's say you have a team of predominantly strong people with a few clunkers thrown in. If you know how to brand that small group and make them look like a whole empire, it shoots your business ahead of the pack, without a doubt. It's like speed for business building – branding.

PR – that piece of branding I used much more than advertising. A: it was free. You didn't have to pay someone to write an article. B: you could take control because you could dream up the stories and send them out there and see if a reporter would bite on them. And C: when *The New York Times* or *The Wall Street Journal* quotes you as an expert, it's far more powerful and convincing than you paying for a full-page ad that's $80,000, trumpeting you as the expert. Nobody believes that, only a few. They think you might be successful because you could afford the ad. But when you're quoted as 'the expert' in a major publication – which happened in my career, day in and day out – everyone assumes you're hugely successful and the right person to go to.

So yes, I used branding – particularly the PR piece, the free piece of branding – my whole life, to the degree that most of the conversations I had in the last five years of my business throughout the day were with reporters rather than sales managers, salespeople, suppliers. I hyper-focused on that because it was where I got my biggest bang for my buck, which was virtually no buck at all. But I got such a big bang for it and it shot my business way ahead of the pack.

Also, it's almost like I stole the stage from my biggest competitors by stealing the limelight. If you steal that limelight, even though your big competitors might be five times your size, the general public thinks you're bigger. It happens every time. If you're bigger, they think in business that bigger is better – unless you're bigger and had a terrible spill and a bad reputation in the press. But bigger, in most people's mind, is generally better and if you look bigger they assume you know more. So all these positive associations happen if you can build a large image. So I was acutely aware of spending most of my time on that.

How were you generating your PR stories? Did you have a team of PR experts or were you having hands-on involvement yourself?

No, I did all that myself. That was, for me, like playing. It was probably one of the most fun parts: that, the advertising, and the party giving, were my three favourite parts of the business. So far as generating those ideas, I found that most of the good ideas didn't come from my sales managers or the brilliant people on the top. I found most of my ideas came from my clerical workers. I would say that was where I got most of my ideas from day-to-day. I knew how to listen.

The other big source of ideas was travelling and play. When I went on a trip, everywhere I looked I got an idea from something: from a bowling ball to a poster, an outfit someone had on, or a new colour. It was about going out into the world and just having fun. I think when you're mentally in that frame, it all works; certainly, it worked for me.

When I was outside playing I always had my big ideas. Always. I never had a good idea at my desk! I could service my business well from my desk, respond, but I never had a creative idea at my desk ever. So I always got people going outside to play and I built that into the company culture as well. I made 'play' a big piece of my company, just making sure people were taking breaks. I would dictate vacations for people who didn't go. I know it's hard to believe, but some people don't honestly take vacations.

So we would force them to take vacations and we'd often declare the company closed. I know we have closed the business, closed it down between Christmas and New Year's every year. A few days before Christmas to a few days after New Year's. I remember initially some of the powerhouse brokers who were then at the company were outraged: "How do we get our services?" Too bad, we're closed. When people came back after that break, especially the support staff – which was roughly one-third of the people in the business – they came back loving the company and feeling refreshed. You didn't have to ask them to work hard; they were just working hard by their nature and so appreciative, sort of "what comes around goes around" kind of thing. So I think those things were key in creating a culture where people wanted to hang out and be there.

Now, fledgling entrepreneurs are often told to step outside their comfort zone and take risks. How big or small do you think these risks should be?

I think risks are key to any business and you'll never meet a successful entrepreneur who isn't a risk-taker – period. Let me think of why that is. I think of risk-taking as being like running a chemical company. Research and development. You have to develop new chemicals, new Scotch Tape, new medication, and they have huge budgets to research and develop. If you're in a real estate brokerage business, nobody has a research and development pile of money to spend. But I saw our company as an innovator and that means doing something first and just trying it out. So we had more failures than we had successes. Trying new stuff is inherently risky because it's new so it's not proven and you can't justify it with your left brain. But if you intuitively feel, "Hey! This kind of makes sense, let me take a shot at it," what you're really signing up for is losing the money if it doesn't work. And I'd say two out of three times things just don't work. They're the best theories, the best concepts. But get it out there in the real world where other factors enter in, it often doesn't work.

So I say it's not so much about intentionally taking risks, it's intentionally trying things all the time and with that goes your money and energy behind it. If you think of all the innovators in every industry, the name brands I'm aware of are usually the innovators. They're often not the biggest company, but they seem the biggest because they're really good at pumping out new stuff. Really good at PR, really good at marketing, really good at reinventing themselves as part of the culture. So I don't think anybody signs up and says, "Let me take some risks." It's really: "What could we think of that's new and what could we try, and let's see what works." Whether that continues in the business has everything to do with whether you're willing to take the failure well.

I had a little trick that I did in my company that really helped – whenever I had someone who would try something new, whether it was a new marketing gimmick, a new sales manager rearranging something in the way the business was usually done or whatever. I had a "fun budget" as *I* called it, or as *they* called it the "mad money budget." So every manager had a certain percentage of their production as 'mad money' that they could spend as they chose. If it wasn't spent by year-end, it was gone – so they had to find ways to spend it. What was also inherently good in that was it said, "I trust you" because you can spend it how you want and you don't have to report to anybody.

What I particularly liked about it: most of the things failed and so when I caught someone failing, I would make a public spectacle of it and reward them. Publicly applaud them and laugh about it and we'd laugh together. So the failing became a part of the culture in a positive way, because this was a hero who was trying something. You have to play that a little carefully because you can't have 15 failures with no success stories. You have to pick them and pace them well. But the fact is it created an attitude like, 'we're supposed to be trying stuff. We're supposed to be out there doing this stuff, and look, isn't it funny?' The other thing is, anything I failed at I made a spectacle of myself too, because if your boss could publicly look like an asshole – excuse my French – then certainly you could too.

In terms of attitude then, failure is all part of the bundle of success.

It's the most important part. You could get a brilliant person who has an idea a minute and most of them good – which rarely happens honestly – but if they can't handle the failure, they won't be back out there trying the next thing. It's too hurtful. Did you ever hear the expression, I heard it years ago and I thought it was so cute it stayed with me, "Asking the girl is the easy part. Walking back to the chair is hard." Can you picture that little man stepping out to ask the next girl to dance? It's really brave, it's the easy part. But walking back *without* the girl, that's hard.

So honestly, with my sales staff, the ability to fail well was the only point of differentiation between those people who did well and those who did not. I'm telling you, I studied my salespeople all those years. They had different styles, different contacts, different ways of coming at the business as well as into the business. But the truth is that the superstars all had the same ability to get up fast. They moaned and groaned, but just for a minute, and they were back up. The people who moaned their way right out of the business were usually the worst people. Moaned and groaned how bad it was, "Oh my god! Did that hurt! Ouch! Ouch! Ouch!" They're talking about the "ouch, ouch,

ouch" on and on and on. Forget it! They took too long feeling sorry for themselves and they just missed the next three sales.

Whereas the winners, they certainly felt the hit like everybody else, but they only gave themselves a minute to lay low and then bounce back up. That's a great gift to have. I think that comes from optimism and confidence that probably you get in the home front, certainly more than anything I could give them. They either came in with it or not and I was not able to nurture that as a trait. That was definitely a trait someone either had or hadn't. I think people got better at it because I publicised the failures so well, but I don't think you could teach people to not injure deep. Some people just injure deep.

It sounds as though you had a winning formula for keeping your staff happy. Did you find then that the word got out and people wanted to come and work for you?

Not initially, not for the first 15 years. In fact, frankly, many of the things we did, we were ridiculed for because they were different from the norm. We had too much fun. People called us the "Corc-ettes." The sophisticated, old-boy network firms thought we were like a born again Christian group or something because we were happy and liking each other. But the laughing stopped once we were blowing by them. And once we were among the two or three most successful firms, they thought we had the magic juice. Everybody wanted to emulate what we were doing. So people started doing PR; people started having parties; people started trying to be silly. Then we were able to really pirate the best people – not all of them but many of the best people – right out of our competitors' firms. Because why would you want to work somewhere and be super successful, if the place itself was boring? If instead you could be super successful and work in a place where everybody's smiling all the time? Where would you go? So it became obvious because my best advertisements of all, my own salespeople, were out walking and talking in the field. It's not like we could keep it secret. The minute they went out the door, everybody who saw them just got it.

So when you were growing up as one of 10 children and sharing a bedroom with your sisters – you were sharing socks from a communal drawer – did you ever imagine you'd be where you are today?

No, nobody knows where they're going. No, not at all. I never had a thought.

When you imagined your future, what did you think it would hold?

All I knew was I didn't want to get married and have a baby at 18, which was the norm in my town. That was pretty easy for me because I never had a boyfriend and you need a boyfriend to imagine yourself having a baby and being like everybody else. For some reason, I just never got a boyfriend – I think I got my first boyfriend at 17. By then, I was only a year away from when most girls were announcing who they're marrying. No, I only knew what I didn't want to do. I knew I didn't want to get married and have a baby, but I had no idea what I wanted to do.

There are lots of horror stories about real estate in the news at the moment. What is your take on this?

I probably sound like a real estate broker, which I am through and through, but I think real estate can never be judged short-term. This is one of the worst real estate bouts we've had or real estate flus or bubble bursting or whatever. Of course, the real culprit is over-leverage on the part of people who couldn't afford it and the real villain here is probably, more than anyone else, the mortgage brokers and the banks who sold a bill of goods to people who really didn't understand the details. They were all told the big lie – the biggest lie in the industry – which is "You can always refinance." But needless to say, when prices dumped down by 35%, people couldn't refinance. They couldn't get out, they couldn't sell. It proved a house of cards. That was at the root of it.

So, is this a terrible time? Yes, for the one in three households in America who have houses worth less than their mortgage. Is that a fun bill to pay every month? Not really. But you can't judge home values over the short-term. I really believe in hindsight we'll look at these days where we have cheap money and cheap prices as the 'good old days' when we should have and could have. But I don't think anybody's going to see that until they look back at it. Like anything bad, you don't see what's good about it until you look back. Both in life and in building a business, whatever, it applies to everything. It also applies to the real estate market. You can't look at where we are now and see it for what it is. I believe we'll all look back and see it as a super sale of the century a few years out from now, but I guess we'll wait and see.

So really, your message to anyone who has bought property in the past couple of years and they're wondering if they've done the right thing, is just hang on in there?

Not even 'hang on', but how about enjoy your home because it's not an investment first, it's a home. We've all got to live somewhere. Would you rather be paying the landlord? Some people maybe, not many people. Most people like to own where they live. Two out of three families in America do. So, why not enjoy where you're living? People are worried about the value of their house daily, people who have no intention of even selling for five years! I think the better thing to do is to think about how you could better enjoy it.

One of the quotes that's about you: "while others talk about stepping *outside* the box, Barbara has seldom stepped *inside* that box." That comes across very strongly to me. Would you say that's a fair assessment?

I don't know what that quote is. What is it?

It's from the President of the World Association of Domain Name Developers, Rick Schwartz. He says: "While others talk about stepping outside the box, which a lot of business people do, Barbara has seldom stepped inside that box."

Oh, seldom stepped inside the box. Yes, because it's boring. You can always do what everybody else is doing and you could even do it much better, but where's the sizzle in that? It's pretty boring. You kind of know before you go into it, it's about as good as it could get. It's a waste of time. I just think you always find the good stuff outside, that's all. You could always hire somebody to tend to inside the box. It's the truth. There are many capable people, but far fewer people who are good on the outside. So that's another practical reason, forgive my practicality, but that's another reason why you're better off. It's a lot more fun on the outside.

More information at: www.barbaracorcoran.com

SIX

Gill Fielding

Gill Fielding is a wealth writer and presenter in the UK. She's famous for her role on 'Secret Millionaire' on TV and more recently appearing on 'The Apprentice -You're Fired'. Gill now runs more than seven businesses and has investments in equities, as well as property, around the world. She left school at 16 with two CSEs.

Q: Gill, your life wasn't always like this, was it?

No, it certainly wasn't. I was born in the East End of London – you know, two up, two down – in the late 1950s. We had no money, no time, no space. There were five of us living in the house, and one of my brothers is mentally handicapped so he was allocated one room all to himself – so the other four of us shared three rooms. So certainly no space, no time. There was no time for me as the youngest child, no money. We had no bathroom, no phone, no television, no fridge, no nothing.

So what actually motivated you in those early years?

I was probably, in retrospect, a lonely child and was left very much to my own devices because my father worked full-time and my mother spent all of her time looking after my handicapped brother. So I was left very much to my own devices, so I was always sitting in the gutter outside the house. First of all, because it was the only place I could get a seat, and secondly, because I was left alone out there and I used to watch the world go by.

So I think I became an observer of life very early on and I was very independent and very solitary and I don't think anything particularly motivated me. I was obviously very self-sufficient. And then when I was about seven, an uncle gave me a five pound note – an old five pound note which probably represented his entire week's earnings because this was 1963, something like that – and I had to hide it in case my parents took it from me because obviously, it would have represented a massive amount of money to them and certainly it was an extraordinary amount of money to me...

We lived in this ramshackle house and there was a cupboard on the upstairs landing. The upstairs landing was dark and scary. This cupboard was called Granddad's cupboard because my grandfather (my father's father) was a rogue, and I think probably that's where he used to hide his stolen goods – so he put the fear into us children to say, "Don't ever go near my cupboard."

So I was sitting in this gutter when this uncle gave me this five pound note. It was a whacking great big blue bit of paper. I knew what it was but I'd never had one and he said to me: "You better hide that just in case somebody wants to take it from you." And I ran into the house, but had nowhere to hide it because I didn't have a room. I didn't have a place of my own, nothing.

So I took the massive leap and ran upstairs and decided to hide it in Granddad's cupboard because it was the only place I knew nobody else would ever look because Granddad would have killed them. I flung open the door, expecting to find dead bodies, etc, and actually found just some odds and sods, leftover stolen goods – you know, vases, books, and all kinds of stuff. I couldn't read at the time so I grabbed a book that was fat, opened it, slammed the fiver in it, threw it into the cupboard, slammed the door shut, and then ran back downstairs.

From that second on, my life changed. There was a paradigm shift on how I viewed the cupboard. Instead of it being the frightening thing, it was now my paradise. Every time I was on my own in the house, I used to go up to the cupboard and open the door and get the book out and flick the pages and watch the blue go by. I set my first ever financial objective at that stage and that was to fill the book out with blue.

It was *The Complete Works of Shakespeare* and the play I had chosen was *Hamlet*. As a consequence, I have built up all of my positive belief structures around that. I know that sounds absolutely barking mad, but if you look at my website, my logo is the watermark that's on a five pound note.

What I've been able to do throughout my life is connect everything to do with money to positive beliefs and behaviours to do with the colour blue, with Hamlet, with Shakespeare. Every time I drive to your neck of the woods, Stephanie, I think about Stratford-on-Avon and I feel abundant and magnificent. So what I've done is I've built up a massive store of positive beliefs about money all stemming from that thing. Now, if ever I need some positive beliefs, all I have to do is connect it to the colour blue or something connected with it and I'm immediately flooded with a sense of abundance.

So did you have any sort of mentor or role model in your early years? How did you make the first step?

I think I was lucky. I think most children are born with, or as young children have, a sense of wonder with money. Unfortunately, our society and our culture, our education system and everything that we come across – certainly in England – is derogatory and negative more or less about money. So from the second that you start becoming aware of money and being glorious with it as a child, your teacher, your parents do the best they can to knock that out of you. We're educated in this country to think that money is 'filthy lucre'. We're educated to think that to talk about money is somehow not a nice thing to do. You know, my mum, bless her – she's dead now but she used to say to me, you know, I say it as a joke – when I left home at the age of 16, my mother gave me two pieces of advice. One was "keep your knees together at all times", and secondly was "don't talk about money".

You know, we are educated to not like money. So when the Spice Girls re-formed, they're sitting on the platform, the journalist said to Posh Spice, "I bet you're only re-forming because you're getting shed-loads of money." I paraphrase. She said, "Nice girls don't talk about money." I screamed at my telly: "Some of us do!" Because there's this whole premise that somehow to be loving of money or joyous with money is somehow a bad thing. It's a British disease. We don't like anybody that's good at anything. We have to knock them down. For example. educationally, culturally… You look at things like Dickens. Mr. Micawber actually said: "Income 20 shillings, outgoings 19, 9 and 6. The result of that is happiness." No it isn't. That's stagnation. What he should have said is: "Income 20 shillings, outgoings 4 shillings, investment rate shillings, you know, buying of property, doing this, doing that." There is never any instance in our educational or cultural history that encourages people to be abundant and to save.

So, 96 percent of our population retires in this country with inadequate funds to see them through retirement, and for some reason we find that acceptable.

How did you manage to break out then from all that brainwashing?

106

I fell in love with this five pound note. Because I was on my own sitting in the gutter, playing this secret game of looking in the cupboard, nobody knew that I was developing this love of money because I was totally unsupervised. I think if my parents had known I was hiding a five pound note in the cupboard and, you know, squealing with delight with it, I think they would have told me not to do it. So I didn't have any of the natural inhibitors because I came from an area where there was no money. Nobody at school had any money. The teachers never had any money. Nobody every talked to me about money. I was able to develop this love with the five pound note and then more money because I got excited by it. I thought 'I'm going to fill up this whole book with blue' and so I then started to try and acquire money so I could get another blue sheet in the book. But nobody stopped me. I think that's the point.

Nobody stopped me because they didn't realize I had it because I was independent, unsupervised sitting in a gutter outside. I think had my parents known I'd got the money, they would have started to say to me, "Oh, Gill, be careful. Don't... You need to do blah blah blah blah. Money is not nice." And I would have started to get the subconscious negativity about it. But because nobody knew I had it and nobody knew who I was and nobody cared about me, I just was able to sit there and glorify and enjoy and build up this massive belief store. Of course, then I became interested in it as a subject matter.

Before I could fill the book out with blue, I discovered something called a Building Society Account. I discovered that they pay you interest and I worked out what 'interest' was. Then I actually worked out things like compounding. I was like, 16, 17, 18, and I can remember at the time I opened the first account. It was a regular savings account where you could put one amount in per month and you've got a high rate of interest and I opened one of these accounts.

I remember joyously saving up a five pound note and waiting on the

Monday morning. I'm outside the building society at 6am in the morning waiting for them to open so I can pay in my five pound and get another lot of interest on it. I was really excited by this and the shop finally opened. I went in and the woman looked at me and she said: "You can't come in today." I said: "Why not? I've got me fiver. I've got me fiver." She says: "You can't come in until tomorrow because you've already paid in one amount this month. So you've got to wait until tomorrow." Because obviously I had breached some condition that meant you could only pay once on a calendar month for every 30 days or something. And I remember going out of the shop and being absolutely devastated because I couldn't pay in my fiver.

But of course, I was back the next day to pay my fiver in. So I've always had this joyous thing with money and I've always played games with it. I do debt destruction tables, you know… pay your bills in the nude. I always have this fun approach with money. I think it's powerful. I think it's sexy. I think it's funny. I think it's glorious. Everything to do with money is totally abundant for me and I think most young kids do have that. But as I say, our society – adverts, advertising, culture, popular culture, education – all knocks that out of kids and I think it's appalling…

So you've got seven businesses now. What was your very first business that you had?

My very first business – well, it's an interesting answer I'm going to give you to that one. My very first business was effectively buying a property when I was 19. I realized I had to do something to accumulate some money because I wanted to go to university. I left school at 16 first of all, by mutual consent (I didn't like them and they sure as heck didn't like me) so I left school at 16 with two CSEs. But then I decided I wanted to get myself educated and knew I needed some money. So the long and short of it was that property really was the first thing. Actually I didn't really get into business seriously until about 12 years ago. Because what I did was I had this big corporate career. I was chief executive of this, and big in the city, and chairman of the Trade Association – all that kafuffle. But while I was working my corporate career, I was accumulating assets on the side – like buying properties, investing in shares, etc etc and I grew my wealth organically. It wasn't like a big thing, but it took me 20 years. It took me 20 years to make my first million. Then in 1997 when I had my final child, I got postnatal depression so I didn't go back to work. I decided to chuck it all in and of course, everybody thought I was mad, crazy, blah dah dah dah dah.

But some six weeks later, I'd got a few nights' sleep and righted myself. I was sitting at my computer – all was well with the world again – and I felt, "Well, okay, here I have a clean sheet. What shall I do?" My first thought of course, as always, was to work out how much money I had and how much I needed. So I always get these spreadsheets and I looked at the spreadsheet and I thought, 'Bloody hell, you know, I've got a million quid here of assets. I don't have to go back to work. I don't have to do anything like that any more.' So that's the day that I realized that I was financially free.

So 1997 is the answer to your question. I set up my first business and it was basically just me writing articles for magazines about money. Then they started to invite me to speak at conferences and so on. So I developed a career then, and that ultimately became The Wealth Company. Of course that now is an international organization that distributes educational products about finance around the world.

How do you manage to keep track of all seven businesses?

Two ways, really. One, I'm just probably *the* most organized person on the entire planet. I wouldn't have said that two years ago because I have always underestimated my own skill set. You know what it's like, when you're good at something, you think everybody's good at it. But my two skills are: knowing how money works and being organized. So I can get 50 things done in a day when other people would do one. That is one of my life's frustrations, is that people don't work at the same speed as I do…

I'm a street fighter, you know. I don't talk about stuff, I just get off my arse and do it. My personality type is that I'm very driven, masses of energy, can get eight things done because I'd rather do something than talk about it.

Secondly, I've put in place a phenomenal support structure. So for example, I haven't been shopping, cleaned a toilet, ironed a shirt, done anything like that for about 10 years because we have full-time support for the family. Somebody's walked in while I've been on the phone here, emptying the bins. So, I've got massive personal support and I've got very strong business support. So I spend my time actually doing important things.

So you delegate the other stuff?

Yes and I delegate the rest. I do a lot of work with joint ventures because I'd rather have 50 percent of something than 100 percent of nothing. So for example, the work I'm doing in America… I'm about to launch a massive brand throughout America and I haven't even got one employee – nobody – because what I've done is I've found another company to do it with me. We're going to split the profits.

So in doing that, I can say our business is all around the world. I can run eight, nine, ten businesses because actually, I don't need to do the bits I don't need to do. I've got a mantra and it's this, "I only do only the things that only I can do. And somebody else can do the rest."

Your philosophy is very similar to Sir Alan Sugar's: that people should just stop moaning and take responsibility for their lives and just get on with it. Do you think *everyone* is capable of being wealthy?

Yes, without a shadow of a doubt. I honestly believe being wealthy is so easy, anybody could do it. It frustrates the hell out of me that we are educated – again, we're back to that subject – we're educated to think that money is difficult, complex, that you'll never understand it.

The number of people that say to me, "Oh, I'd love to be wealthy, but I would never get my head around it. I wouldn't be able to give the time to it." You don't need to do that. What you need to do is to change your brain to say: "I understand this." So for example, most people or the average person in this country spent (I've heard rumour), £13 a week on The Lottery or lottery scratch cards or games of chance. They understand how to do that and they even understand that they've only got a one in 14 million chance of winning anything.

With the exact same money, I can guarantee 100 per cent, people could be millionaires because with the exact same money, saved regularly over a working life, it turns into 1.225 million. So I could educate everybody in the country to be millionaires by the time they retire just by saving their lottery money. Now, that would solve the country's crisis because people would then be able to have a pension because they've got these million pounds stashed away. So all three of my kids have already got a fully funded pension, so my kids are already all right…

I get lots of people coming to me wanting advice and guidance and whatever. But what they're coming to me for generally is the wrong thing because there are two things you need to become wealthy. One is the facts, figures and the tangible stuff like: what interest rate am I going to get, where do I put the money, and all that stuff. The other thing is the belief that it's possible, the belief that you can understand it, the belief that you can do it. Most people – 99.9 percent of people – come to me thinking that what they need is tangible information. But it isn't. What they need is the intangible. So I have a very bizarre career – because all of the stuff like being in charge, being an accountant and being the financial expert, etc is what gives me the credibility and why people want to come and talk to me. But actually, that's nothing. You could learn all that off the Internet. You could get a book and learn it in a week. What's important about what I do is the intangible. It's the belief and showing people that it can be done, and of course the biggest example I've got of that is myself. I know *anybody* could be a millionaire in their lifetime because I've done it.

Now, you've stated that the opportunities for business at the moment are "more magnificent than at any other time and there has never been a better time to start a business or develop a great idea." Lots of people might be surprised to hear this. Can you explain why you feel this?

Yes, there has never been a better time for the main reason that any already established business in this country is having difficulties – because every established business in this country is carrying overheads. So there is a business cycle. So every business goes through expansion, contraction, maintenance, you know, it's a cyclical thing. Companies don't stay flat. They grow a bit, contract a bit and whatever. And what the opportunity is now is to get on to the business cycle, get on to that wheel, in the 'just about to grow' phase. Because all the people that are already big or established are now going through a contraction phase.

So it's about getting into the right place at the right time. So for example, if you want to – let's have a thing. Let me think about it. I don't know, a plumbing business. Right. An existing plumbing business that's established has got half a dozen staff. It's got an office girl. It's got maybe small offices. It's got somebody answering the phone. It's got an advertising thing that runs in the local newspaper etc, etc. Now, if they're going through difficulties, they've got to reduce something. What companies tend to do is cut out customer care, because it's an overhead. But by cutting out customer care, they then start to produce a shoddy service. You, as a new entrant into the market place can give your time to customer care and giving exemplary customer care, generally at a cheaper price because you're not carrying the overheads. So absolute perfect opportunity...

Your philosophy is that there are three lanes of the wealth motorway. Can you go into this in more detail for anyone who is unfamiliar with the idea?

Sure. There are three main ways to become wealthy. That's to be invested in stocks and shares or other people's businesses via shares; to be invested in property; and to be invested in your own business. I think it's important to say first and foremost – you will never be wealthy having a job because all the job is, is just over broke. All you ever do when you're working is cover your current spending habits. So a job has to go by the board and I think that's a tough thing for people to hear. But you'll never be wealthy while you're working. So you have to be invested in the three things that over time, will produce enough money for you to be financially free. The good thing about the three lanes of the motorway is that if you do it right, it will accumulate for you without you putting in any effort. That's the whole point is to make your income passive: so to be invested in shares, stocks, other businesses, your own business, and property.

And over time, since God was a lad, curiously the rate of return from the stock market has been almost identical to the rate of return from property, so they both have grown over time. They double every seven to eight years. So actually, if you look at those two together, you can see that there's some sense in being invested in those particular two lanes. Although they grow at the same rate, since God was a lad over hundreds of years, they obviously grow at very different rates on a daily basis. We tend to find that when the stock market is having a good time, the property market isn't having such a good time. Or we get times like now, where actually, neither of them are going through very good times. But with pound cost averaging and long-term investment, they both will equal out to doubling every seven to eight years.

The other thing about those two as a pairing is that they are different risk profiles. Property is fairly low risk and it'll chug away – chug, chug, chug, chug, chug, chug, chug – and gradually builds up in value. Whereas the stock market, as you well know, it's a bit wooh-wah, wooh-wah, wooh-wah. It's all over the place. It's up in the morning, down in the afternoon. So actually, by investing in those two different lanes of the motorway, you're accessing different risk profiles and protecting yourself in different ways.

Many wealth gurus talk about taking risks when creating wealth and stepping outside your comfort zone. You take a much more balanced approach, don't you? And you believe it's important to have a balance in your portfolio and have much more protection against risk.

Yes. I'm very risk averse because I'm a wife and mom. I've got three kids, five cats and a goldfish, so I'm very risk averse. But people look at me and they say, "My God, you know, you're taking a big risk there." I'm not, because what I do before I ever invest in something is I collect my evidence and – unlike people who invested in Madoff or whatever – I collect my evidence properly. The more knowledge you have, the more education you have, the more evidence you have, the less the risk is. But you're right. I do take a very balanced view because I didn't want to make my money in the way that the vast majority of self-made millionaires do. Self-made millionaires on average lose their money twice before they learn to keep it. I'm sure you've got all those statistics. So people like Jeffrey Archer: they make it all, they lose it all; they make it all, they lose it all. I didn't want to go through those peaks and troughs.

For me, wealth has always been an organic growing thing. I found that by taking appropriate risks and with appropriate knowledge, I've been able to take this steady approach to growing my wealth. I take much more risk now, but of course, I've got much more to fall back on. I mean, when you've got 500 properties or something, it doesn't matter if you make a Horlicks with one. But if you've only got two properties and you make a Horlicks with one, you've got trouble. It's obviously self-evident, but I don't think I take the risk at all.

You've got three children. How have you managed to combine your home life with your work life? You must have a very, very busy day.

I do but unlike most working mothers, I was able to take my child to school this morning and I will pick her up. I'm able to go and watch every show. I'm able to drive to see my children because I haven't got a job. I have more time with my children than, you know, an average parent because I don't have a job. Anything that's vaguely important to them, I'm there watching on the sidelines. I'm with them. So I've just spent a month in America – basically doing part-business, part-holiday. The whole time I was in America for that month, I had my kids with me. Because I've got the money and I've got the time.

And of course, I've got a full-time carer and various nannies who help them with their homework at times where it's needed, etc, etc. No, it's interesting that one, isn't it? People think because you're busy, you don't have time for your children – but actually because I'm busy, it enables me the opportunity to be with my children when it's relevant. So you effectively can cherry pick. So I don't, you know, comb their hair through for nits or anything like that. Somebody else does that, but when it's important that I'm there watching the show or the sports day or something, I'm right there.

You were on the 'Secret Millionaire' programme on TV, which shows millionaire benefactors going undercover in deprived areas. Tell me what happened during that programme.

Well, I can honestly say to you Stephanie, that bloody programme changed my life. It did really. Because I went into it thinking, "Oh, TV programme. I'll zip in, do my fortnight, then bugger off home and that will be it." You know, I went into it thinking I was just going to zip in with my cheque book. I mean I knew I didn't want to just give away to people and then forget about them. I knew I wanted lifetime projects – and they are all lifetime projects and I'm still in touch with all of them. So I went in and met these people, and for the first time in my life I trusted my instincts. Because up until then, I had always done this 'evidence, analysis thing' blah blah blah blah blah.

When I was there, it was funny. I got there. I was scared witless. I mean the TV company dumped me in this place about 10pm at night with a £10 note in my hand. So I had no money, no phone, no idea where I was. I couldn't shut the door properly. It was dark. There were bangs and crashes outside and I thought people were shooting each other. I was absolutely petrified and the TV crew zipped off into the night and said, "Bye, we'll be back tomorrow." So I basically did what any working class girl would do. I started cleaning. So I cleaned the bits of the house I wanted to live in, then basically barricaded myself in to a tiny room at the back until daylight dawned. I mean, that's the state I was in. I got up the next morning and got myself a job and by the end – after 24 hours – I was feeling fairly relaxed and the TV company allowed you to earn £10.

So one day, I earned £30 but they took £20 away from me because they wanted you to be absolutely rock bottom. So I earned £10 and when I got home – I got back to my little hovel – I'd done a bit of budgeting. I'd bought something for my supper and I had £2 leftover. So I thought, 'as a lark I'll pretend I'm investing this'. Because back to the lottery example, with the million pounds: £1.85 a day is all you need to become a millionaire. So I thought, "I know. As a joke, I'll put my £1.85 or my two £1 coins in a sock and pretend that it's me investing."

Then the next day, as I zipped off to work and I was going diddly dee deedly dum diddly dee. I was happy now and I was cleaning tables and I loved it. Honestly, I was as happy as Larry there and if I haven't got a family, I think I'd still be there. Those tables have never been so clean. I had a wonderful time and of course, then on the way back, I decided I had enough money with the £2 I had from yesterday. I managed to save £3 on Day Two so I turned it into a £5. I turned it into a 'blue' and you will know immediately what that did to me. It kicked me into an abundant mindset. Then, I started to do budgeting about what I was going to spend. I was going to buy one packet of pasta and that was going to do three meals and all the rest of it. Then I found my bed and it was late on the second night and I could see over to Canary Wharf. The sun was setting behind Canary Wharf and I was sitting there on my bed, budgeting what I was going to do with, you know, 73 pence. Then I put the paper down and I laughed because I thought, "You silly tart, what are you doing? You know, this is a TV programme and you're working out how to make money from 73 pence. Then, I put my pad down and I burst into tears because I knew exactly what I was doing. I knew at that stage – I knew the secret to wealth because I had innately started to create it all over again. From that position, I would have been a millionaire again in 18 months or something. Because I can do it much quicker the second time around, because I've got the benefit of knowledge and experience and belief because I know it's possible. I sat there crying looking at Canary Wharf, thinking: 'Jesus Christ, this is *massive*, because I *know* how to make people wealthy.'

It was the first time it really, really hit me at that cellular level what I know. Because up until about 10 years ago, I thought everybody knew. And I burst into tears. That's why I started to write *Riches, The Seven Secrets of Wealth You Were Never Told*, because it gave me such a sense of belief, such a sense of contentment, such a massive boost. Because I now know it doesn't matter what happens to me: I can be destitute, living on the streets of the East End of London, working in the café, and it will be fine because I'll make it all over again. So I then had my own private agenda while I was back in the TV company – to work out the first steps of how to do it. Over the phase of the two weeks, I earned a total of £99 and by the time I had left, I had a business idea going. I had £85 invested effectively in a tax-free ISA, and I was working out how to make money from property. So I had all three of the lanes of the motorway going again within the two weeks, starting with nothing. It was massive, Stephanie. It just kicked me up a whole new level.

And more recently, you've been on 'The Apprentice – You're Fired'. What about that? You obviously see a lot of people on here who are trying to learn about money. What do you feel about the people that you met there and the mistakes they're making?

First of all, I will say, 'The Apprentice' outfit and the people involved with it, it's the nicest TV I have ever done and they're charming. The candidates on a one-on-one basis are all wonderful, you know. Listening to the people when they come on the 'You're Fired' show, they all seem like normal human beings. The problem is – and I know this myself from working on a reality TV show – is it's the most unreal environment you're ever in. So they all behave like idiots, don't they? I mean you can't believe the fundamental mistakes they make week in, week out. But my excuse for them is that they're working on a reality TV show and your mind just goes to mush. The problem with your mind going to mush in that kind of environment is that you've got no structure to pick yourself back up again. Whereas if my mind goes to mush – like right now talking to you… There's a plan to what we're doing and there's a plan to what I'm writing and there's a plan to what my business does.

So as soon as my mind goes to mush, I can just go back to the plan, go and have a cup of tea and a biscuit, talk myself out, come back, look at the plan and get going again. Trouble is with working on 'The Apprentice' is that there's no plan. There's no plan other than to provide entertainment – so when their mind goes to mush, they've got nothing to bring themselves back to. So I think the lesson I would bring out of that is you need planning. You need discipline.

You've been working with Nightingale-Conant to create wealth creation products. That sounds very exciting.

Well, Nightingale-Conant as you probably know, are the largest distributor of personal development products in the world, so I just have an agreement with them. I mean, their European CEO saw me speak at a conference and said to me afterwards, "Anything you want to produce, I will distribute." So whenever I get the time to sit in a recording studio and put some of this down on disc, he publishes it for me. So, that's absolutely fantastic and my story CD, 'My Daughter Wanted a Pet, So I Bought Her a Greyhound', was Nightingale-Conant's biggest seller in Europe last year…

So how have you learned over the years about things like marketing, and client retention, and hiring and firing people?

My philosophy in life is that I still don't know what I'm going to do when I grow up because I'm still learning. So I am a very inquisitive person. It's probably one word, I'd put for it – I'm very good at spotting the things that make a difference to the outcome. I think people generally are very bad on that. You know, the famous quote: 'if you keep doing the same thing and getting the same outcome, it's a definition of insanity.'

I'm very good at spotting the things that make a difference to the eventual outcome. As a consequence, I've learned what's important and there's very little that's important to be honest. In terms of things like marketing and personnel, it's treating people the way that you would like to be treated yourself. I know that's a bit of a truism, but it often amazes me when I speak to chief executives and they talk to their staff like they're idiots. What they're doing when they do that is they're setting the template for the way that the staff speak to other members of the staff – and more importantly, how the staff treat the client. So if you want your staff to speak to your clients well, you have to speak to your staff well, because that's when you set the template for the communication.

So things like that... I think the way I've been able to do it, is strong leadership and back to this being very organized and just getting off my bum and doing it. I remember I was chief executive of a financial services company and I had a call from the head of the distribution area that was like sending out all the policies. She said to me, "Oh, we're so behind with the policies, we can't keep up. We can keep up with them coming in and putting them on the computer. But whenever the policy documents come out of the machine at the end of the day, we haven't got time to put them in envelopes and dispatch them off to the clients. We're weeks behind and blah blah blah." And I said, "All right, get some temps in. How many temps do you need?" And she said, "I don't know." I said, "All right. Well can you work out how many you need. Judge how long it's going to take?" And she said, "Oh, I'm busy. I'm busy." So I strolled down there. As the chief executive, I went into the post room to find this pile of policies in the corner. I thought, "Right, I'll do half a dozen, time myself, and work out how many temps we need to clear the backlog." Well, you know what I'm about to say: I cleared the backlog before I went home!

Because I just *do* it. No prevarication, you know. It's a thief of time – prevarication. Just *do* the sodding thing. I'm very down to earth...

It sounds as though you're very, very organized. You're very methodical. You assess things very carefully before you venture forward. Has it all been plain sailing for you?

Now, that's always a difficult question because people are always saying to me, "What's the biggest mistake you've ever made and, has it all been easy or whatever?" Two things I want to say about that is: increasingly, it gets easier and easier. It's not because the economy is easier, because the economy is not easier. But I think I'm now using more of my instinct and intuition, and combined with the financial stuff, that means that I'm going at a faster pace and it's easier.

The other thing I will say I must have made some of the weirdest mistakes ever. Particularly with property, people always say to me, "Did none of your properties ever go wrong?" The answer is, "Yes, it did." You know, I had tenants who kicked the door in and broke the windows and all the rest of it, just like everybody else. But I've never ever let it get me down. I've never ever let it hold me back. I genuinely have seen only challenges and not negativity. I know that's going to sound really bizarre but I must have really strong filters. Because if you said to me, "right, name a problem that you've had or something that you found difficult", I'd sit there for ages going, "errm, errm – can't think." Because it's all been accumulated in my brain as a learning experience. That's all positive and it's all eventually worked out.

Now, if somebody came to you today saying that they want to turn their finances around – they're in a terrible mess financially – what advice would you give them? What would be the first thing that you think they should go and do?

The secret to happiness financially is understanding your income and expenditure flows. That is number one. Very close behind is understanding debt. They are the two things. People say to me, "Oh, you know, I can't look after money. It's terrible. I need your expert opinion." And, you know, years ago, I used to sit down with people. I'd say, "All right, okay, what's your income and expenditure each month?" "I don't know." When you get people logging in *exactly* what comes in and *exactly* what goes out, that is often enough for people.

These people used to come back to me and say, "Now I've done that income and expenditure thing that you told me to do, I now realize all of our money goes on take-aways... or my husband buys wood... or you know, I buy a small branch of Boots every time I go out and it's all on the bathroom shelf." When people understand their income and expenditure flows, then they can then generally see how to turn it around pretty quickly. Of course, once you put into people's minds to see that everything that comes in doesn't have to go out actually. You could actually keep some of it and invest some of it. Once you start planting those kinds of seeds, people do tend to get it. Record your income and expenditure. I think it is the easiest thing that I do are on a daily basis – but I've got people that I've been working with for a couple of years, who still can't do it. "Oh, I can't do it because my husband buys the shopping." Well, keep the bloody receipts then! You know what I mean? People will not control their income and expenditure because they believe it's difficult to do. So we're back to the old beliefs thing again.

But number one, control your income and expenditure. Learn *exactly* what comes in and *exactly* what goes out to the penny and then you'll be in a better position. And secondly, learn the difference between good debt and bad debt, and what debt does to your credit score. So get to grips with debt. They're my two top tips.

The top mistakes that entrepreneurs make when setting up a business? What would you say that those are?

Delusions of grandeur. Without a shadow of a doubt, there is one mistake people make every single time when they set up a business. People will come to me and they'll say, "I'm going to set up a business, and I need you to give me some guidance." "Yes, ok, yes, what are you going to do?" "I'm going to set up a hat shop and I've got these lovely business cards made in the shape of a hat. I'm going to have a blue one and my colleague is going to have a red one and we've even found desks in the shape of a hat. We're going to do our advertising here and we're going to get paperclips made there…" What about the bloody business?

But what they do is they have these delusions of grandeur. You don't need a business card in the shape of a hat or a desk in the shape of a hat. You don't even need a desk or a business card at all. What you need is to run the business! So those delusional things that people *think* they need in order to start a business – like bloody hat-shaped business cards – are nonsense. What that does is it creates overheads – that's O-H-O – and that's a problem with businesses, too many overheads.

What's a typical day like for you? Many people think that millionaires lie around on sun loungers all day and have their meals fed to them by servants.

Well, I have meals cooked for me – so that bit's true. I don't lay on sun loungers because I don't want to. The thing is, every single day I live my passion and first of all, I'm incredibly lucky to know what my life mission is. My life passion, my life mission, what I'm on this planet to do is 'light the spark of financial possibilities for people'. That's why I was born in East End and that's why I am who I am, etc, etc. So not only do I know what my life mission is, I get to live it every single day. I mean, what better life can you have?

And the glory about what I do is when you live your life on mission, everything goes at double speed. Decisions are easier, things happen quicker, money flows quicker, profits are greater, sights are clearer, sounds are sharper, everything. When you live your life on mission, right on the edge, you can see the whole world and everything is easy. So my life is easy because every single day, I get up and I say, "Right. This interview – is this going to enable me to light a spark of financial possibility in people? Yes it is, so I'm going to do it." I don't have to sit there and say, "Oh, should I do it? Do I know who she is?" I don't have to go through any of that crap that drains people and that takes everybody's time away. "Does this light a spark? Does this enable me to light a spark?" Yes, it does. Yes, I'll do it. So decision-making is incredibly quick. So every single day, I do exactly what I want to and that's living my life mission.

More information at: www.thewealthcompany.com

Rachel Elnaugh

Rachel Elnaugh is an entrepreneur, an author, a speaker, and a business mentor who became famous while appearing on the TV show 'Dragons' Den'.

She founded the gift experience firm, Red Letter Days, from her front room when she was 24 years old. It went on to generate a turnover of a £100 million in the 16 years she ran it. She was awarded the title of Champion for Entrepreneurship in the UK by the International Association of Book-keepers in 2008.

Q: Rachel, you shot to fame on the TV show 'Dragons' Den' as the sole female entrepreneur on the original panel. Do you think women have a different perspective on business than men?

Definitely yes, I do. I think women tend to run business from a passion and with much more collaboration and integrity than men tend to. I think a 'feminine' business, if I can put it like that, is a very different way of running business which is just as powerful as the old kind of 'alpha male' style of capitalism, which actually we're starting to see die.

Do you think that women in business face very different challenges than men?

I personally think that women in business have got a huge opportunity that isn't available to men because most consumers are women. Seventy per cent of customer decisions are now made or influenced by women, so I think businesses that are run by women which have got that passion and integrity and social conscience, are the ones which are much more likely to turn customers on. Actually, I think the tables have turned, because when I started in business back in '89 probably the men had the upper hand. But I think from a marketing point of view, 'feminine' businesses are much more attractive to customers.

What about things like labeling? For example, a man might be 'gritty and determined' and that's seen as a positive quality, whereas in a woman that's given a very different label?

I think the thing with women in business – and I certainly knew this when I started out – was that to get along, you had to be as hard as a man and you had to prove yourself. You got sucked into a kind of 'alpha female' state of being very assertive, very determined, very tough, very scary, and people thought of you as a walking bitch. I think that was very much the case maybe 10 years ago, but now things are very different. I've met so many hugely successful entrepreneurs who are very feminine, and who are not a soft touch or a pushover, but they are successful in harmony with their femininity rather than trying to fight against it and pretend it doesn't exist.

So, doing things on your own terms?

Yes, I think having the confidence to dress in a feminine way, rather than in a navy pinstripe suit or whatever. I do think in that respect – and I don't want to be horrible about Deborah Meaden – but in terms of the role model that she presents to women in business, it's quite archaic, this sort of scary pinstripe suit image with black stiletto heels. Even Deborah has softened her look in the more recent series of 'Dragons' Den'. I think women can be delightfully feminine and still be very successful and not feel they have to compromise their femininity to get on.

You founded Red Letter Days when you were just 24 years old and it went on to generate a turnover of a £100 million in the 16 years that you ran it. Tell me about the early days of your business and how you got it started.

Well, really the idea was: what do you get the man who has everything? My background has been in accountancy, and in particular in dealing with the taxation of entrepreneurs and small businesses. So, I thought when you went into business, it was just like turning on a big tap and money flowed out and it would be very easy. I was very quickly proved wrong and it took a good 18 months to get the business off the ground. It was so tough. Suppliers wouldn't even speak to me. It was really difficult to engage people. I was just 24 years old and a woman, and so it was difficult to get people to take me and the business seriously. So, it took an awful lot of energy to get that business off the ground.

As you say, you were a young woman in your 20s. You had no track record. It was an unproven industry at that time. Your family and friends were telling you to go back to accounting. You were also at one point a single mum of three young children. What on earth gave you the courage to keep going?

Well, I think as an entrepreneur, one of my greatest assets is the ability to manage my own motivation. So no matter how bad it got, or how depressed I got, or whatever 3 am crisis 'dark nights of the soul' I had, I was always able to re-energize myself and get back into battle the next day. So, I think just being persistent and never giving up and having blind faith was what got me through. I had a lot of self-belief and I really knew that the business could work. I was relentless. I kept on and on and on at it. People who wouldn't speak to me in Year One, I'd go back to in Year Two. Then maybe in Year Three, they'd deal with me and only with *one* product. Then in Year Four, maybe they'd give me *all* of their products. So, I was relentless and I think I just ground everyone down at the end.

Red Letter Days went into administration in 2005 and the remaining assets were bought by your fellow 'Dragons' Den' judges, Peter Jones and Theo Paphitis. How do you feel about it now looking back?

Well, the interesting thing is that Red Letter Days, since it went into administration, has generated cumulative losses of something like £10 million. I think that goes to show that there was a much better deal that could have been done that didn't have to destroy the business in the process. I think when you push a business through administration, it's very damaging to a brand. It's such a shame because had Peter and Theo backed me, we'd probably have floated by now and they would have got their money back five times over. So, I just think that the way the insolvency laws are structured, to provide a real incentive to push a company to administration rather than save it, quite often work against the interest of British business. That's my view on it.

What else have you learned from the challenges that you faced with Red Letter Days? Is there anything you would have done differently if you could have your time over again?

Yes. It's an interesting question because people keep saying: "Oh, how could you have faced it?" As though losing the business was the worst thing that could ever happen. At that time, I thought that was the case

– but looking back, I now realize I had to go through that process and I had to lose the business to take me to where I am now. I think it's very easy to lose sight of the fact that life is actually a journey. Sometimes you outgrow things but you cling on to them for far too long. I think that that business was taken away from me because I had to move on to a new role. I think life was leading me in a new direction, but I was holding on to the past, and I think sometimes life makes the decision for you. If you don't let go of your own accord, fate intervenes. So, actually losing Red Letter Days has taken me on a really fascinating journey. It's 4 years ago and I've done so much since then. It's been such an interesting time. So I don't know if I would change anything actually.

My husband sometimes says: "If only you'd sold the company, we'd have millions of pounds and we could just be on holiday the whole time." But I say to him: "I don't think that's what the universe had in store for me." I don't think I was ever destined just to sit on the beach for the rest of my life because my work now is far too important and if I had millions of pounds, I probably wouldn't have done all the great things I've done over the past four years. I'd never have faced my fear of public speaking, I'd never have had the incentive to help so many other entrepreneurs, and I certainly wouldn't have had the incentive to write my book *Business Nightmares*.

And especially with the times that we're in now, and all the people that you can help.

Well, exactly, because that's the interesting thing. Everything over the past 4 years has led me to work in the enterprise sector – helping other entrepreneurs on their journey, which is now one of the biggest growth sectors in the British economy. So, it's a strange, strange path that we're sometimes led on and hopefully I *am* helping people. There's a lot of people out there who absolutely do need that kind of encouragement, support and guidance.

You've had many more experiences than the average person could cope with. You were fighting to save your business right up to the birth of your fourth child. You were then back at work within hours and having to breastfeed your baby between meetings. Your home was put up as security in an attempt to save your business. How did you cope?

Well, it's interesting, because I was trying to refinance the company when nine months pregnant. I remember on the Friday, I struggled up to see one of our biggest customers, who had a huge contingent liability. So I went to see the finance director and I was so heavily pregnant. I just said to him: "Look, you have got to help us. You've got to help sort us through this, because otherwise we're going to crash and I need your help." And this guy was so angry with me, and he wasn't interested in doing any form of deal or negotiation.

So, I struggled all the way back home and went into labour on the Sunday night. I had the baby about 6 am on Monday morning, was wheeled back into the ward and sneakily switched on my phone to see if there had been any messages. I immediately got a call from the *Daily Mail*, which I accidentally answered. They said: "We want an interview – what's happening?" And I had to say to this guy: "I'm really sorry but I'm in hospital. I've just had the baby." Of course, this was the worst thing to say to a *Daily Mail* journalist because the next day in the newspaper, it came out, "and she was *even* back at business in her hospital bed just hours after giving birth." Like I was a terrible sort of mother!

So, the media fall-out was quite an eye opener. But I just think when you're in that kind of tunnel, you just go through it and you roll with whatever you have to deal with. When you're so determined to make things work, you do whatever it takes. Really, I should have been in hospital that week to be honest. I shouldn't have been out in meetings. It was ridiculous.

When the whole thing crashed, the saddest thing for me was being betrayed by some of my staff and the people who I thought were friends who went to the press and slagged me off. I realized that they were just 'fair weather' friends who had used me during the good times and that was quite sad.

Yes, it is. You now run a business rescue service to help other entrepreneurs who are struggling. What's the most important piece of advice you can give to help get a business back on track?

I would say the biggest single issue is that entrepreneurs leave it far too late. So people will call me for advice when they're days away from meltdown. It can take a good three months to refinance a business, or restructure, or do something with it. So, I would say to anyone whose got problems, you have to take action as early as you can because leaving it too late is always going to be a disaster.

So what are the best ways to instantly improve cash flow in a business – because this is going to be something that's very typical at the moment.

At Red Letter Days, we released something like £3 million cash into the bank within weeks just through simple things that sound really obvious. It's very easy for businesses to get out of touch with simple things, for example, like collecting on invoices that are out there. Most businesses have got a debtors' list, where they could get a very strong credit controller to relentlessly collect the money they're owed or take legal action to get the money. In normal circumstances this might annoy customers, but if you're on the edge of financial meltdown, it's much better to annoy a few people and collect the money and survive, than be nice to everyone.

Also, you can renegotiate terms with your suppliers – rather than paying suppliers within 30 days. I can think of a firm that changed ownership, and immediately they changed their payment terms from 45 days to 90 days literally overnight. The message was: 'If you still want the business accept the terms, otherwise we'll go to someone else.' They were quite ruthless.

And I think there's lots of expenditure in businesses that is unnecessary as well; you can also look at cutting costs.

What sort of areas?

Every area. You just have to sit down and go through the profit and loss account and see where the money is seeping away – is it on 'nice to have' items which aren't adding value or are they essentials? So, really just stopping all expenditure on anything that isn't absolutely core to the business. Most businesses should be doing that as a matter of course, but quite often businesses just get lazy.

It's very easy to get into cost cutting mode. But I do also think you have to be really focused on marketing and sales. It's so easy to cut back and think: "Well, we won't do any more marketing." But you've got to keep driving the business and keep marketing and keep selling. There's a price to pay if you think you can stop all of your marketing activity. A lot of businesses go into this negative spiral of not driving sales, which is always a disaster.

You're currently entrepreneur-in-residence at the British Library Business Centre where you're holding master classes for entrepreneurs and you're teaching magnetic marketing techniques. As you say, isn't marketing one of the first areas to be cut when a business is struggling?

Well, it can be. But I think that's usually because most businesses don't understand what marketing truly is and they're maybe not leveraging low-cost marketing techniques to their advantage. There are lots of simple and easy and effective ways to drive sales without having to spend *anything*. For example: search engine optimization; social media; PR; driving word of mouth; giving customers incentives to recommend friends; upselling. Lots of ways. Most businesses are sub-optimized in marketing terms. So, there's masses you can do without having to spend any money. Many businesses I go to don't even have a customer database. They have no communication strategy for their customers at all. So, simple things like that, which can be high impact quick wins that don't cost the earth.

Customers, it's often said, are your best form of marketing. Would you agree with that?

Oh, absolutely yes. Obviously, a satisfied customer is not only going to buy from you again and again, but is also going to recommend you to all their friends. So, keeping in touch with existing customers, letting them know what you're up to, what your new products are, encouraging them to refer you to people, rewarding them to refer you to people are all good strategies. All really simple things you can do without it costing a fortune.

Now, branding. You were a pioneer of the UK's £250 million experience gifts market. What are the main ingredients for creating a market-leading brand such as Red Letter Days?

I think the key thing is you have to think like a market leader. From a very early stage – well before we had any size at all in fact – we set up stall to say that we were the number one. I think when you take the mental position of a number one, your whole thinking is around innovation and driving the market. Whereas our competitors tended to just follow what we did – so automatically, if you follow what other people are doing, you're not the number one. You can't be, because your mental attitude is basically copying other people and so it makes you lazy. So by having that mental stance of being number one, and taking the position of really wanting to be innovative – constantly driving the market, constantly improving, constantly pushing business forward – no one could really catch us.

You built up your business from your front room on a shoestring budget. Would you say it's possible for *anyone* to do that?

Yes, absolutely. Particularly now, with the Internet. People can create businesses from a laptop anywhere. You don't even have to own any product. You can just sell other people's products through affiliate links. So, I think the Internet has opened up a massive opportunity for *anyone* to set up a business literally overnight and start creating money instantly. The set-up costs are so minimal now, barriers to entry are non-existent for most businesses, and it's a really exciting time. You can take an idea from conception to completion and get it live and up and running within 24 hours. If it doesn't sell or it doesn't work, you can change the whole site or close it down. Business is so interesting and very powerful at the moment.

What would be your advice for somebody who is just starting out?

I would say to people, absolutely to follow your passion. It's so easy in business to think, 'Right, I'm going to go into mobile phones because there's loads of money in mobile phones. Therefore, even though I don't know anything about mobile phones, I have no interest in mobile phones, I'll go into the mobile phones business.' The problem is, if you take that approach, you might be successful but you probably won't have much fun doing it. I always think that if a business is based on your passion, it becomes a sheer joy to work on – because it never feels like going to work, because all the time you're doing things you love and you're so passionate about it. Your energy is infectious. So, I would say, have the confidence to follow your passion. If you put that at the heart of your business and give people great things – whether it's products or services or experiences – that is the best foundation for a business.

What about monetizing your passion? A lot of people have passions that might not be, or might not seem immediately to be, financially lucrative?

Well, I think you have to create a business model around what you do, that basically yields profit. I think women in particular, have a tendency to undersell themselves. They're apologetic about asking for money for what they do. I think you need to get over that mental block and create packages out of your passion – whether that's a product or a service or an information tool. If you put the right business model behind *anything*, you can make profit from it. Unless of course, there's absolutely no demand for what you're doing, in which case, if there's no demand for what you're offering then you haven't got a business anyway.

And what are the most common mistakes that entrepreneurs make?

I'd say the number one mistake is building in far too much fixed cost and overheads into a business early on. Like maybe getting an office, maybe spending lots of money on infrastructure or brochures or products and stock, before you've even tested the market. Because the one key thing that I've found with businesses of my own and others is that you have to keep trialing and testing and adapting and adjusting. If you suddenly just order 10,000 brochures and you find out after giving out 500 that none of them work, you wasted your money on the other 9,500. So, it's far better to do a really short run of things and buy small amounts of stock. See what sells and what doesn't – because it's not always the thing that you can think will be a sure-fire success. So, for every 10 things you do, or maybe for every 10 products you sell, one or two might be brilliant sellers, three or four might be average and the other five or six might be duds. But most people make the mistake of focusing on the five or six duds that don't sell. They say: "This business isn't going anywhere." But if you're really smart, you'll just focus on the one or two that did really well and shed the other eight and then try

10 more things. By focusing on the bits of the business that are doing well and shedding the rest, over time this will give you a fantastically successful company.

So, testing. You've got to continually test your products and see what the response is?

Trialing and honing and seeing what works – that applies to every part of the business. For example, if you go to a networking meeting tomorrow and meet 10 people and get their business cards: of those 10 people, eight of them will be of no use to you whatsoever, but two of them will become really brilliant customers. But you won't know which those two are. So, the 80:20 rule can apply to products, it can apply to marketing. You might try 10 different forms of marketing and find that eight really don't work and two are brilliant. You've got to keep trialing and testing and honing and see what works.

You offer an entrepreneurs' profiling test on your website. Do you think most people have a good idea of what their profile is already or are they surprised by the results?

I do get lots of feedback from that test and most people really agree with it and say: "Wow, you got me down to a tee." Except for the Execpreneur. The Execpreneurs are typically people who come out of a corporate environment where they're used to doing things by the book. They're the ones I always get a two-page e-mail from, explaining all the reasons why my test is wrong and why they're not an Execpreneur. I think, 'well that's exactly what an Execpreneur would do.' Because if you were, say, an Alphapreneur, you'd say: "I couldn't give a stuff what Rachel thinks. I'm going to do it anyway." You wouldn't write a two-page e-mail complaining. That's quite funny really.

So, how did you put the profiling test together?

I created it out of my own personal need to become a better consultant and mentor. I realized that if I could understand what makes people tick, where their comfort zones are, how strong their drive and energy is and where they're working from, it would give me a much better picture of the person and what they can achieve and the best way to achieve it. So really, I developed it as a personal understanding tool. I wrote it myself through my experience from working with entrepreneurs and in addition, the types of needs of people that I was constantly meeting. So, I developed my 10 categories based on the archetypes of people that I'd met.

So, that helps people to assess what their abilities are, what their strengths are, so then they can delegate the tasks they're not so good at to other people?

Yes. So just understanding the dynamics of how they work and how that can be detrimental for them in business. For example, a Safepreneur is someone who might say they want to be rich. But when it comes to the crunch, they won't leave their salaried job and they won't invest any money, and by the way, they haven't got any self-belief and they didn't think it could work anyway. And if you've got that kind of low energy and are very risk-averse, business really is not for you. You'd be far better to maybe buy a franchise, or a ready-made business, or just stay in a job working for someone else.

So, I think it gives people a bit of an insight because statistically, only 5% of people who go into business are hugely successful.

That's incredible, isn't it – 5%? That leaves a huge percentage of people who are working really hard but don't get to that level of success.

Something like two-thirds of all businesses fail in their first two years. Usually it's because people just give up. Of the 33% that are left, the majority of them are just surviving, without it really working for them. Of the original 100%, only 5% will really hit on something that works and grows and have great profit. So it's a very low success rate really.

With these odds, why do you think that so many people chase the dream then? Because it is their dream, or I should say, their passion?

It's everyone's utopia isn't it? You see Peter Jones and Duncan Bannatyne, and you see the Ferraris and you hear the success stories. But what most people don't talk about is the challenges and the disaster stories behind the scenes. People underestimate the sheer amount of energy it takes to breathe life into a business. Unless you're highly motivated, with high energy, highly passionate, highly charged, very assertive and very relentless, you'll probably fail because there's so much stacked against you. The people who've got the tenacity, persistence, determination and self-belief to push through every obstacle that pops up – the people who are relentless and knock down every wall – those are the ones who succeed.

But if you're going to be the kind of person to give up and be ground down with every obstacle and objection, you're not going to get very far. So those are the challenges that sort the men out from the boys.

Did you have a business plan or a mentor when you first started Red Letter Days – or was it just a matter of trial and error?

I do recall creating some business plan, which was totally ridiculous and didn't materialize in any shape or form. But when the business took off, it actually happened through me meeting a marketing guy who was a real guru, who really helped me. When the business took off, we learned very quickly that it was far better to run with the opportunity and go with the flow, than to try to second-guess what was going to happen. We had no template. When you create an experiences company from scratch and there's no one in that industry, how do you model that business? How do you model how your sales are going to work? How it's going to morph? Or suddenly, the fact that it went into retail – we didn't even see that coming. So, I think sometimes running with opportunity is quite a good way to build the business in the early days. Later on, maybe, you need to get more structure and strategic approach. I think when you're growing, it's a case of: "the answer's 'yes' and now what's the question?"

In the past, you've described yourself as a bit of a rebel. Do you think that quality is essential for entrepreneurs and business people?

Yes. People who are mavericks do make quite good entrepreneurs because they're willing to go against the grain and be bold enough to be different. Most people tend to want to comply and conform and fit the norm. I think people who are prepared to be innovative and daring and different, they're the ones who are successful.

You were brought up over your father's electrical store. He warned you, didn't he, against going into business? He said that you'd be making a rod for your back. Why were you drawn to business in spite of him?

The thing is my dad ran the business and he lived above the shop. Every day, he went and opened the business. Every night he closed the business. He managed everything. He managed all the staff. He was the classic sort of entrepreneur that works 'in' the business, not 'on' the business. Of course, because he never built a team around him, a) the business wasn't scalable, and b) he could never have a day off.

And so, I think when I decided to start Red Letter Days, I wanted something which wasn't just all about me because I could see that was very restricting. So building a structure and a machine and an operation that could run without me having to be there, I think was the difference between me and my dad really.

So, it didn't put you off seeing him struggling or tired?

No, not really. I think I just learned from watching him that when I went into business I didn't want to run a shop where I had to sit behind the counter every day. My dad ran a great business, but I think things were different in my era of the 1980s with big businesses building and women floating on the stock exchange and having the kind of vision to think, 'Wow, I wonder what I could do? How big I could make it?'

One of the talks that you give is titled, Surviving the Recession, and then another one is, What Tomorrow Holds for the UK Economy. What's your take on the economic climate at the moment? Obviously, the newspapers are full of doom and gloom.

Well, my personal view is that this isn't a recession. I think that this is a massive period of change where old style 'alpha male' capitalism is polarizing against the new way of doing business which is much more feminine, collaborative and socially charged. And so, I think what we're seeing is a huge tension between the old style corporates desperately trying to preserve the status quo and a whole new wave of businesses which are very agile, very transparent, very socially switched on, very ethical, and very passionate about what they do. They're using the power of the Internet to overtake and outsmart all of these big dinosaurs. We're already starting to see the fall of some of the big corporates like the banking giants. Other big businesses are really struggling and I do think that we're in a massive period of change, after which business will not be run in the same way that it has been. I think the old-style capitalism model was totally unsustainable in every aspect.

You recently gave evidence to Parliament on how to develop an enterprise culture here in the UK. What advice did you give?

Well, I work a lot in the enterprise sector and I go to speak at events and a lot of these are sponsored by government bodies. It really feels like the message is: "Go into business. Everybody go into business, set up your enterprise, be your own boss." Blah, blah, blah. But I think that if we're going to pump millions into encouraging enterprise, we need to be really strategic as a country about which sectors are the growth sectors of the future. We need to align all of our resources, support, grant funding, training and all the rest of it into specific sectors which are the sectors of the future. So for example, sustainable energy or biotechnics or nanotechnology or even alternative therapy and health – rather than encouraging people do any old business, perhaps creating more retail products no one needs. It doesn't feel like there's any strategic direction to the country's enterprise policy.

And what are your plans for the future? What does the future hold for you?

Well, I do have some big visions for the future which I try not to share because the media always comes back to haunt me. But I've been doing a lot of personal empowerment work and thinking about what I want to achieve in my life. I think when you get past 40, those sort of things start becoming pressing don't they, when you've only got so many years left to go. I'd like to do something international. I'd like to do something around personal empowerment, and I've just set up an events division where I think a lot of the work that I'll be doing in the future will be about arranging empowerment events for entrepreneurs. That's a whole new departure for me, but it feels like the right thing for me to be doing at the current time.

You talked about empowerment. Are there any rituals that you do every day like visualizations or affirmations or list making?

Well, I wouldn't say that I do them religiously every day because I'm not the sort of person that does a routine, but I do try to spend a lot of my time on input. I try to meditate as much as I can, and I do spend quite a lot of time thinking and writing affirmations and statements of how I want things to be.

It's so easy, isn't it in business to get sucked into doing, doing, doing – clearing e-mails, and sorting out this that and the other, and rushing from A to B. What I tend to find with most entrepreneurs – including myself if I'm not careful – you just end up on constant *output*. If you don't have that *input* time, if you don't have that *still* time of thinking, contemplating, planning, stepping back and thinking, 'What do I really want to achieve and what's going to help me get there?' you can end up like a very busy fool. I see a lot of entrepreneurs in that trap of thinking, 'this is not going right. I'll just throw more effort at it.' In fact, what they should be doing is stopping swimming and going with the flow, wherever that takes them.

Or doing some sort of strategic planning?

Well, sometimes just stopping and having stillness allows you to receive wisdom about what you should be really doing. So, if you're swimming against the flow, you're not getting very far. If you can just stop swimming and get *in* the flow and go *with* the flow – not only will it be effortless, it will be great fun and you'll get forward a lot faster.

Finally, how would you like to be remembered?

I'd just like people to say: "Gosh, you really helped me." In whatever way I touched people – whether through being their mentor or even if they're just reading my book, that I really helped people on their own entrepreneurial journey.

More information at: www.rachelelnaugh.com

EIGHT

Teri Hawkins

Rev. Teri Hawkins is an international speaker. She's also a leadership coach, entrepreneur, author, and an ordained Unity minister. She was paralysed after a car accident as a teenager – and doctors said she would never walk again. She defied their diagnosis to become a world-class athlete and a millionaire by the age of 30.

Q: You've been described as "a genius in bringing out the greatness in others." Tell me a little about your coaching and the retreats that you hold.

If I have a genius it is that I believe in the greatness of every individual ever born in this world. The only way I know to get people to see their own greatness is to give them an experience of it. One of my gifts in life is that I love to learn. The more I learn the more I've realized that the answers to my life questions are inside of me. Instead of giving people knowledge or teaching people what I think they need to know or do, I create experiences so they are more likely to find answers from within their own genius. I've always worked very diligently at creating those experiences because it is how miracles happen and I love miracles. They are everywhere all the time, every minute. However, we don't become conscious of our miracles by reading or taking a test, they come to us through experience that changes our view of our moments. It just seems so much better if those experiences can be had without the trauma or drama. So, the more I have practised creating experiences for myself and others, the more skilled I have become at it.

You mentioned that you think "we've become cogs, duplicating the thoughts that we've learned from the machine of our upbringing." Can you explain what you mean by that?

Every society is put together in a certain way to produce a certain outcome that follows the values of the leaders putting that society together. Every society has a certain way of doing things and they consider those things the 'right' way of doing them. Each country is different in what is right and what is wrong and each country is willing to kill to defend their belief. Which means people would rather kill than accept other ways of "being" as okay. This is how deeply we have become cogs. In order for the machine to keep doing what it's always done and keep producing what it's always produced, it needs the 'cogs' (or the people) to keep behaving, reacting, believing, spending, the way they've always been taught. This is what causes us to stop thinking for ourselves. Therefore each of us is given rewards, pats on the back, and welcomed in society according to how good a cog we are. If we follow our dreams, or be who we have always wanted to be, we're no longer in the machine and the machine needs us there. That is why societies have made it sound so difficult, so risky, so ridiculous to follow our dreams. It's not complicated. It's really quite simple. People will either break away from the machine to discover a different life than cogs are supposed to experience, speak for themselves and make the difference they have always wanted to make. Or they'll be the good little boys and girls and good little men and women, do what they've been told and taught to do, and keep doing it. I like to teach cogs – and we all have 'cog' in us – how to live as the individual they were born to be.

At what age would you say that you actually broke away from being a cog in the machine?

I don't think you can ever completely break away, but I think the dedication to live in that process began when I recovered from my paralysis. I realised that all the medical doctors – and what they said – did not know more than my own wisdom. When I walked again and against all their diagnosis expertise, it broke this illusion that someone could know more about my body than I did – even a highly educated someone. That's where it began for me.

Tell me about that time: you had an accident didn't you, and then went on to become a world-class athlete?

Actually I was an athlete before and that's part of the devastation of the accident, is that my real dream and the only thing I felt I was great at was being an athlete. How coggish is that? When I was paralysed – contra-lateral by the way, right arm, left leg – I reached the ultimate assurance that I was indeed worthless. If I was not an athlete, I had nothing to live for.

It was a car accident. The paralysis was diagnosed as permanent. I dragged my left leg around like a wooden-legged pirate and my right arm was useless. It was the college volleyball coach that created the experience for my miracle to happen and she wasn't even my coach at the time – I was a basketball player. She took me through a detailed visioning, about where I would be in five years and had me tell her everything I saw, felt, heard, even smelled and tasted as I followed where she led me inside my own brain. I was coaching girls' basketball – she asked me about the basketball players and their attitudes, what they were good at and what their weaknesses were. She took me through games, a season; and into the state finals. She talked to me about our offence and defence; even what the lights were like in the gym; what I was wearing; what the opposing coach was wearing and doing; how was I going to win; and she even took us into a tense overtime. I was there, living what I was seeing, feeling, thinking, being in that visioning.

In the midst of it all, she suddenly asked me: "Teri, wait a second. I need to know, are you walking?" I was. In my vision, 5 years in the future I was walking. Something clicked. I can still remember the feeling in that moment of the reality happening inside my head. It was more real than the reality I had been fed about my dismal future according to the experts. That's it. I knew I'd walk again. I never doubted it again. Approximately 10 months later, I got my arm back. And a few weeks after that, I got my leg back.

Wow – that's amazing! What were the doctors saying to you throughout this time?

What happened was my neck was completely inverted and my autonomic nervous system, a sub-nervous system, was damaged as well. So my neck was inverted and it was pinching off a key nerve to my leg and my arm. There was just nothing they could do about it other than try to break the neck and reset it – which is not something you do. They were just basically telling me I was a paraplegic, that's it. That's pretty much what they were calling me. I was going to be paralysed for the rest of my life. That was a done deal for them. They were through diagnosing me long before I recovered.

So you learned a very powerful lesson then that helped you through your life?

Without a doubt, lots of lessons. One of them, of course, was visioning

– going inside, trusting yourself. Belief… faith… whatever you put your faith and belief in, it will be your reality. Lots of things came from that. My whole perspective in life changed. Even though I came from poverty, I never saw that as a bad thing again. I saw it as key to who I was and am now. And when people have made absolute statements to me, it's like: "You know what Teri – nothing is absolute unless I believe it."

Did you always think you'd be as successful as you are today or were there other hurdles along the way?

No way. Not even close. My life desire truthfully, my biggest dream, was to be safe and to be sure that I didn't die unloved. If I did that, I considered that to be a really good life. Maybe that is why money has never been a concern for me – because it wants to be a party to love and belonging as well.

What was the changing point? What was the turning point?

I've got to say the turning point isn't so much that we instantly start walking in the other direction, but that we turn and the whole view in front of us starts to change. Hopefully we continue to turn and take different paths and when we make a bad step, we just turn again and take a different step. But really, surviving the paralysis was what woke me up. In all my years of speaking on it, writing in my book about it, everything else, I can't even begin to convey what it's like when your entire reality is turned upside down. That's basically what happened. It put me in a different direction. I just didn't even see life as the same colour, texture or path that it had once been. My recovery was the first of many of these experiences.

And from there, there were a lot of other things. I was a thief and a professional con artist for some while. Leaving that was not like the day that I walked again, with immediate realization of a great event happening to me. I did not suddenly become a person that knew how to make money honestly or how to change lives. There was no one moment of realizing I was now a help to society and good in relationships. This experience was more the result of constant little steps. Still the absolute desire for that change, to become a "good person", to love and care for myself was possible because of my healing from the accident.

In your own life you went from experiencing lots of hurdles, and then to being a millionaire by the age of 30. How did you achieve that?

How is a good question on that, isn't it? We always want to say: "First I did this and then I did that, followed by this other thing and a bit of this as well." We want to find out the format, or outline for how we got to where we are. But I think I got there like the fleas. You put them in a jar and put a lid on it. They jump and hit the lid, jump and hit the lid, jump and hit the lid. Eventually they get that there is only so high they can jump without banging their little heads. Then you take the lid of the jar off, and they will not jump out. They have been taught the limit and even without the lid they will no longer test that limit. They will remain in the jar. That is what happened to me. The lid of the jar came off before I had hit my head too many times – either that or my recovery simply turned the jar upside down and shook me out.

For me, the sky is the limit. I completely believe anyone can do anything. I don't just say it because it sounds good or to get people to buy books – it is simple truth to me.

I believe money came to me early on because I stopped holding back from people the truth of my darkness and shadow – and mine was ugly without a doubt. All of us have darkness. I always will, I know that. We just choose whether to use it or not. I am nakedly honest about all my selfishness, blame or other darkness that sneaks in to my thoughts. I seem to give people permission to be okay right where they are. By really being okay right where I am – and never expressing that I am in any way perfect at all. How I made my millions? I made my millions because that's what being the best me I can brought me. Because I did what I love doing and I never did it for the money. I loved what I was doing and money wanted to be a part of the life I was living not just the work I was paid for.

Did you have a mentor along the way?

I did. I had several mentors along the way. The most complementary and touching to me was Og Mandino.

How did you find your mentors?

I didn't really – it was more that they found me. I'm mentoring a few people now and it's quite a funny reversal because I wonder if my mentors – my two main mentors are no longer alive – if they felt the way I do. My feeling as a mentor has been curiosity. "Ok, you want me to be your mentor. Why? What is it you think I will be for you?" I found my mentors I think because I was open and receptive in an attracting kind of energy. They wanted to be around me and they felt that they could help me, and they did – in countless big and small ways. Without the one I would never have walked again and without the other I would not have discovered my genius with people.

What about somebody else who might be looking for a mentor? How would they go about finding a mentor? How would they know they'd found the right person?

I think anybody that wants a really great mentor has to stop talking all the time and start listening. You have to really listen with your heart, listen with your ears, and open up your mind to the fact that everybody in this world loves to help other people, and hopefully that you do, too.

You just open up your mind to it and visualise what it would feel like and be like, and why do you want to mentor. I do believe sometimes people want a mentor because they think that the mentor is going to solve their problems, and that's not a good idea. It doesn't work. Truly, I believe what mentors do is they are tough on you, but they believe in you and you can count on them. They are the ones that will say things others won't. But they're also the ones that will believe in you when everybody else doesn't. My mentors saw all of me and did not take credit nor blame for the actions, mistakes and successes I experienced.

There's just some kind of chemistry. We all kind of know when we meet a person that's really going to be a great friend of ours. We kind of know a person with potential to be our partner in life. I think the feeling when you find your mentor is a bit like awe – you're a little awed by them. They're not better than you. You're just awed by them – something in them really pulls something out of you. You're there to listen to them, not to try to get what they've got. Just to listen, that's the biggest thing. Oh, and don't select a mentor according to the amount of money you think they can teach you to make. I suggest you select a mentor by how well they push your buttons and bring out the courage in you to let go and create inner change.

You've talked a little about the low points of your life, what about the high points? What would you say the high points have been?

One of the greatest high points in my life, without a question or doubt, is all the beautiful kids that are in my life. And my husband. I have a phenomenal husband. I think one of my greatest successes is I have a phenomenal marriage. I didn't get married until I was 40 and my husband is in no way, shape or form intimidated by anything you might label as my power or abilities or anything else. He is completely and totally supportive of what I do. We laugh a lot together. I don't try to change him. I work every day to be a better communicator and show my love more. I'm just fortunate that way. I have phenomenal friends, just the greatest people. All my friends agree that without me in the picture they probably wouldn't be friends with each other because they're so different. And I have a lot of kids in my life. I was, and am, very involved with the kids of my close friends, and like a family member in their life.

My kids, friends and husband are such a high point for me. Nothing is better than being with the people I love and trust. It's the reason to live and the glory of life. Whether I have one dollar in my pocket or five million, what matters to me are the people I love. That sounds like a 'coggish' answer – what we would all say – but it is my truth.

What does 'wealth' actually mean to you? A lot of people when they hear the word 'wealth' think of dollar signs and jingling money, what does it mean to you?

What it means to me without question or doubt is freedom to give. I love giving to people who give to others. In fact our foundation – Our Own 2 Hands – is about just that. We give to those that inspire us by their giving to others. We are not about giving to charity out of a sense of pity or need. We give to individuals or organizations that inspire simply by their giving. When someone gives to someone else, not out of responsibility or pity, but because they want to give – whether to a company or a person – that is inspirational. We then want to somehow recognise, give and support them.

The whole joy of having a lot of money is the freedom to *give* and to be in that flow of the universe. That's big for me. It's such a joy. It's such fun. It's like playing in a sprinkler on a hot day, or sliding crazily down a snowy hill – it's just fun. The "weeeeeeeeee" kind of fun. That's what money gives me – whether I give a $1 or I give $10,000 – it's fun.

It sounds as though it's back to that thing of: even if you weren't paid for it, this is what you'd want to be doing.

Yes, it is. I've always said to people: "do what you love". I have said to myself from the time I came back from the paralysis: "Make this a good day to die." I want to be able to say when I die; I want to be able to have that last conscious feeling of, "Teri… good job." The other thing I say at night when I go to bed is: "Would I do what I'm doing for a living right now, for no money whatsoever?" If the answer is "yes", I stick to what I'm doing. If the answer is "no", I'll change it the next day.

Are there any other rituals that you do every day?

Yes, at night I do 15 minutes every single night of forgiveness. I take my day, the day that I have just lived. I don't try to deal with huge, big things of the past, just today. I visualise my day. I go through my whole entire day and I forgive every little thing. Every little thought that was inconsiderate, every little thing that pushed my buttons, I just forgive little things, myself and other people and everything else. I say to myself things like: "I forgive myself for not treating my body better and drinking more water today. I forgive myself for getting upset by the lady who pulled out in front of me. I forgive myself for getting irritated at the guy that had 45 things and got into 'five or less' in the grocery store. I just let go of the little things. I forgive my brother for this, my mother for that, the stranger for that. I just do that for 15 minutes, that's all. Every day. I have done that for many years. That's a real ritual I never stop doing.

The other thing I do every day as a ritual is I spend time with my dogs. I can't say I do it every day because I travel and sometimes they're not with me, but I miss it if I don't have it. Animals are very healing energy for me. So I spend time with my dogs and my cats every day just being in silence – no electronics around me, nothing else – just walking and being with them. Those are two huge rituals.

Then I have a real sweet one. Since the day I married my husband, we never part or go to sleep at night or leave each other without kissing each other goodbye. Never, not once. Not in 12 years.

That's lovely. These are the sorts of things that you teach people – forgiveness as an important habit and practice, and gratitude – on your retreats?

Yes, and my book *Life Retold* gives people permission to enjoy forgiveness of themselves and others. My retreats are very interactive. People don't come to just listen to me. There's a lot of nature involved, I bring people to Central Oregon. It's an opportunity for people to not just have four, five or six days of a retreat – but to take something found inside them with them when they go home, so the retreat stays with them. It includes nature stuff, a lot of laughter and fun, music. I get people involved with simple stretching for the body, mind and heart. I like to do simple, fun things and make sure people really have an internal peace that goes with them for the rest of their life. They don't have to keep doing a bunch of retreats that are huge and long. They can instead kind of take the retreat with them like a constant internal vacation, if that makes sense.

If someone came to you today wanting to turn their life around – if they have had similar hardships to you whether illness, poverty – what would be the first step you would suggest? What would be the first thing you'd tell them to do?

I think the very first thing if someone came to me and they were in that position is I'd probably give them a hug. I'd probably look at them in the eyes and I'd say: "If I can give you one thing, I'd just let you know where you are *right now* is so perfect. It is so perfect. You are such an incredible miracle in life." If there's anything I could give them right there, it's the moment, it's the second of knowing that they could be safe and they could be okay right where they are. It's a journey, it's never one thing. If I can do anything, if it's a smile or a kindness that helps that person feel better about who they are, I'm all in.

I've got to tell you, Stephanie, a story that was powerful for me. I was a chaplain at Leavenworth Prison for a very short amount of time, but it was a profound occurrence for me. I asked on my application to be sure that I did not do any counselling or work with anyone that had harmed children in any way or if they were incarcerated for any sex crimes of any sort. Somehow that got mixed up, and what I got was exactly *that*. I got child molesters and I got sex offenders. I couldn't believe it. I went in on my first day and thought, 'Oh my gosh, what's going on?' Whether you believe in God, Allah or whatever divine energy in the world – I believed fully that there must have been a reason this happened.

So I did my job, I listened to these people, even though they had committed in my mind the worst crimes that you can possibly commit. I would kill for a child. I'm that way. The innocent – children and animals – I feel that we are all responsible for them. For me, I sat there and listened to these people and I had made them out to be such villains. I'm going to tell you: they love their family, their friends. There were a few really mentally ill, I know, but I did not get many of those convicts. They love their mothers. These people I had labelled as 'creeps', without redeeming value, had kindness and goodness in them. I no longer just said the words to sound wise, I really *got* that no matter how horrible the things are we do, we all have that light in us somewhere. We all have that good. They were where they belonged – they belonged in prison. But it didn't mean they were all bad. That was a great learning for me.

You're right, there's always goodness in people no matter what. That was again a really important lesson?

I tend to be a person that has pretty dramatic lessons. I think I'm a little stubborn. No doubt that's why I teach it. When I decide I know something, when I decide this is good or that it's right, it's just about the time the universe slaps me in the face with a cold wind saying: "Teri, listen to me, you will never have all the answers." My ego hates that, but my higher consciousness has experienced it enough to be able to hear the wisdom of it.

Going to the practical side of things... somebody who for example might have watched Rhonda Byrne's film, 'The Secret'... they're doing the gratitude exercises, they're thinking about their passions, but they still feel that they're not making their breakthrough. What do you think is holding them back?

Because I was healed through visioning, I will start there. One of the things that happens when we start talking about visioning is that we don't get all of the senses involved. From a practical standpoint, I believe that if you're truly doing visioning – and not just playing mind games with yourself – you need to experience not only sight but also taste, smell, sound, feel and emotion, in your vision. You want to be totally in the vision using your senses. Once you start engaging the senses, the mind doesn't know any difference between the vision and the true physical reality of this moment.

When it comes to visioning I have experienced a lot of people playing mind games. They're trying to see if visioning 'works' and wanting to prove they are right, that visioning really does or doesn't work – and that won't work. You've got to believe in the vision as much as what you see in front of your face every day. That's why adding the senses to your visioning matters. If you're not having fun and you're not really feeling it, then your mind is playing some pretty dirty tricks on you. Because truthfully, visioning will work 100% of the time if you can truly sense and be present in the vision. Visioning does not have hope in it, because you are living it, no hope needed, it is reality. Visioning always, always, always works. But you can't keep testing it and saying: "Why hasn't it worked?" If you do that, you are just starting back at zero again. In fact, it might be before zero because you're putting that doubt in the universe. Once that happens, it doesn't matter how long you've been doing the vision. The minute you start saying: "This isn't working," or "This doesn't work for me" or " I'm not sure this is going to work" you're way before ground zero. We've got to get back to the point of being open and willing if our vision is going to manifest into our physical life. We cannot pretend with our own beliefs, because they are in our own head, and we cannot lie to our Self and expect our Self to believe the lie. What you believe is what you are living. It just is not more complicated than that. Visioning is a vehicle to change what we believe and the physical world will follow. If visioning has not worked for you it is because you have never experienced visioning.

How did you learn to run a business and manage money? Obviously, there are stories about the people who win the Lottery and then they lose it all a year later. How did you learn about the more hands-on side of things?

I did lose my first million, my first five million. Then it came back again. How did I learn to do it? I do have a practical side to me. I don't spend as much money as a lot of people with a lot of money do. I live in a fairly modest home. What I did is I really started dedicating my life – thanks to Og Mandino – to giving. I don't mean sacrifice, I mean loving to give where I am inspired. So I don't keep buying. I don't have a lot of homes and a lot of stuff and that kind of thing. People wouldn't walk into my home and think, 'My God, this is a multi-millionaire,' they wouldn't do that. I'm maybe upper middle class in what my home looks like. I like nice things, I'm not saying I don't have some but I don't keep buying them. I think that kind of helps because then money becomes something that frees you to give rather than something that you need to have in order to buy. I think that's huge for a lot of people, why they lose their money. They're in it for the money instead of in it for what they love and let the money follow that.

They're trying to work for money. Personally I believe money would be a horrible boss to answer to.

Most people in the United States are taught that. I think in most of our western countries they are taught basically: work for money. And we never work for money. If we do, it will keep leaving us. Money is just an energy and it doesn't want to be chased after. It wants to be able to be a currency, to be free. So for me the real big thing of why I've been able to be successful financially is in being someone that's practical and learning to give. And I have never worked for the money. Never.

Do you think that's an important lesson for other people when you're talking about people's bad relationship with money – or how they've been brainwashed into thinking that they have to work in a certain way?

I think it's very important. I think your relationship with money is just a reflection of your relationship with everything else in life. I do absolutely, positively believe that happiness and enjoying life in every breath you have is really what life is about. It's such a gift. When people throw it away, chasing after money, it's sad. It's really sad. My grandparents never had a lot of money and I think they were the richest people I've ever met.

What about your parents and their attitude towards money? Your father left, didn't he, when you were younger?

My dad left in a weird way, he'd leave and come back, and leave and come back. It was very damaging to our family. I had a very dysfunctional and poverty-centred home life. My father was a rogue, a con artist. I have a mind much like him. It's probably why I went into being a con artist myself. My dad left us, and my mom worked very hard to keep a roof over our head. She's an amazing woman because she came from an era where she couldn't get paid nearly what the men did. But she did what she needed to do, she worked hard and she fed us. It was a very difficult upbringing, but then again we all have those stories. We can either live in them or we can use them as a foundation to create better, more loving, fantastic stories.

Do you have brothers and sisters who you grew up with?

I have brothers. I love my brothers. No sisters whatsoever. We're not as close as we used to be but I would absolutely do anything for them. In my eyes, they're geniuses and they're the reason I'm such a great athlete. They're the reason I have a college education. They gave so much just by being great big brothers when I was growing up. If they did something, I got to do it. They taught me as they learned and treated me like a boy – what other way did they know? The social skills I got from them continue to serve me in countless special ways.

Tell me about some of the people that you've helped and worked with over the years.

I don't think I've changed any life. I think that I've put myself out there as much as possible to be there when people are ready. I mean I can work with someone until I'm blue in the face or they're red in the face – the decision is still always theirs. How many times have we helped people and they go right back to the same thing because our desire is to help them? I can't take the credit, I really can't, I mean it. That is why I provide experiences rather than knowledge – because it has to come from the individual. I am more a catalyst than a teacher I suppose. I love to see people blossom, but until they're ready – it doesn't matter how great you see yourself as a teacher – nobody learns a thing unless they decide to.

I do hear often from my clients that with me they feel okay to be who they are – good, bad and ugly. From that, they have opened their minds to follow their true dreams instead of following the dreams they are supposed to have. Because of that many have been able to go out and give to others in the way they've received.

It sounds as though what you're saying is that if something feels like hard work, you're not going to succeed in that.

Yes, I like that, I really do. If you don't love what you're doing, if you're doing it for the money – and this is what I guess entrepreneurs do all the time. They work their butts off all the time, they sacrifice so much: moments with their children or their family or with nature or their animals or whatever it is, or themselves or a book for goodness sake. They tend to do that because they're chasing after some thing. Really, right now, this moment – right, right, right now – if you're doing something that you can't find joy and love in, I'm thinking it's not going to bring you what you want – certainly not money. I mean if you were money, would you want to hang around that?

Would you say that's the number one mistake that entrepreneurs make?

Absolutely. That and they fall in love with their passion and their dream. They want everybody else to fall in love with their passion and their dream. Then they want to keep dreaming in all of this, and they don't want to focus in to do the things that need to be done in order for that dream to happen. Then they do so many different things and get burned out, they don't get everything done. You've got to enjoy it. Even when I used to read my financial reports or organise how I was going to make some calls for selling something, I loved it. I enjoyed it because I kept the dream of what I loved, and the difference I wanted to make, in the forefront of my mind all the time. So I loved all that stuff, even made games out of them.

So how do you turn your passion into something that's a winning idea?

It is a lot of work. I'm not going to say it's not, but it's fun. I do not intend to be esoteric all the time. I am also quite practical and down to earth and want to give you some definitive answers. But this is real to me. It works, always. I have to be real in what I believe. It's not like there's a magic button and there is no 'get rich quick trick' – at least not one quicker than what I have previously said. Living your passion is fun, always fun. The process is the fun. If it isn't fun, you have been way-laid. I think it's partly that I never worked for the day that I'd arrive, or the day that I'd get some place. I worked for the day I was in and I loved it. I think a lot of people say: "I'm going to do this and this and this – and *then* I can do this, and *then* I can have this." I don't think I ever really did that. So, I'm not sure if I am answering your question very well because I think the passion *is* the winning idea.

What drives you, what's your motivation? Someone might say, "Why do you want to go out and help all these other people, Teri? You've got a fantastic life. Why don't you just go off and spend time with your family?" What drives you to get up every day and help other people?

What else is there in life but to be who you are? That's who I've chosen to be. I do spend time with my family and I do give a lot. I don't think I'm driven. I think that I'm pulled through life by my passion for life itself: for living animals, for our beautiful earth, for the amazing unknown. I've just been kind of pulled through life and I just go ahead and follow. If I had to pull life or push life, I think that'd be pretty hard. I guess what gets me up is one smile on one face that the moment before wanted to cry; or one child that doubts himself, that in the moment of laughter realises life is fun and exciting. Or one older person that's walking down the street; I meet their eyes and see the wisdom and the kindness in them. I mean, what else is life for but those seconds and those moments, and the best way to have them is to be active in life. That's it.

Man, I'm truly giving you all kinds of esoteric answers. You ask what drives me? Well, I don't know. I have no clever answer. I suppose the love of life itself and the fuel of living my passion.

It sounds as though you have that child in your heart and you see beauty everywhere, even in a blade of grass.

Right now as I'm talking to you I'm sitting in my car. There's a little bit of rain, a little bit of mist in my window. Right out of my window about 10 feet away is the most beautiful Ponderosa Pine that's being blown about. The leaves are being blown, so these long pine needles are all blowing one way. The pattern it makes, it's got about five different colours of green and gold and yellow in it. Then, it calms down. What in this universe created that? It's just amazing that that life lives. It's just astounding to me. Beautiful.

You're also a Shaman of the Animal Lore, can you tell me about that because that's a very different thing to coaching leaders.

That's often the difficulty with entrepreneurs – we are often multi-talented or multi-faceted. We have to focus in or nobody can figure out what we do. Where I'm at now is I don't try to figure out what I do, I let it all out there. Then when it seems most appropriate or effective, I go that way. My shaman background, I'm a Shaman of the Animal Lore. Basically I'm a storyteller of the animal lore; I find a great deal of wisdom through animals. My grandmother was of the herbal lore. I find a great deal of power in the animals.

Just when I walked out of the door to find a way to connect with you via phone, right in front of me there was a rabbit. So I took a deep breath and I just let go. I said: "If Stephanie and I are meant to talk, we'll talk. We'll have the time. If not, then it wasn't meant to be and that's okay." I'd gotten tense because you have all these preconceived ideas: 'I told Stephanie I'd be here. Then these phone problems happened.' Prior to seeing the rabbit my inner voice confirmed, 'you've got to find a way to make this happen.' You can get caught up in that so quickly and so fast, and here's a rabbit right in front of me. That rabbit to me instantly was a message. I took a deep breath and I said: "there's nothing to be afraid of, nothing." In my Native American training, rabbits have a real strong thing around understanding fear. It's not that they're always fearful, but they understand fear. If you're aware of that, you can make a choice with it rather than letting it control your life. So that's what I did, and here we are talking on the phone as planned, even if the plan on how to connect changed.

As for other people, I oftentimes sense an animal energy around people. Maybe I'd send them a picture if I know them, or something similar. But I often say, if we're in a conversation: "Do you have a thing about tigers?" They'll go: "Oh my gosh." That's a release of some of their feelings or something like that. I can't say I use it actively in my life as much I used to. I do it a lot more for myself when I'm in meditations or walking with my dogs. It's part of why dogs are so important to me, as horses were – and still are. I love horses, but I don't live with them any more. Part of the reason is that dogs have such a feeling of devotion. With my upbringing being fairly unsafe in many ways, I've always been attracted to that emotional safety even though I'm a risk-taker in so many ways. I like that feeling around me. My husband is that way, a very devoted person who I feel extremely safe around, and dogs make me feel that way as well. That's a bit of how my shamanic awareness inserts itself into my life.

One of the things that struck me is that when you talk about being a professional speaker, you say your skill is not in speaking but in being a listener. That's quite an interesting way of thinking about it.

It is, and it's the hardest thing for me to get speakers to grasp. They want to get me on the phone for 30 minutes or they want to come and work with me for two days and have their whole life changed, and suddenly make lots of money speaking. People don't have enough attention span for us to speak at them. The whole thing of a professional speaker is a misnomer. It doesn't work. People need to be involved. As a speaker what we have to be able to do is *hear* an audience that never talks to us.

Right now, we have a lot of lay-offs going on in companies. If I was back in the business, I would want to help those left at the company after lay-offs. I would want to increase productivity – maybe even enough to bring some of their friends back into the company. If I want to do that, I have to first listen. I can't go in thinking I have a solution. It's not my world. I'm there to listen and provide experiences so that they can pull something different out of themselves and out of their thinking, so they can act differently and thus have a different result. Even when I'm speaking at a keynote, my job is to hear the audience.

Think about it. If you were at a convention… say it's the fourth day of the convention – it's seven o'clock at night and you've just gotten through eating dinner. Do you have an idea of who these people are, just a little bit? If it was a convention, all about technical stuff and everything else, you have more of an idea. How much energy will they have for sitting in seats and retaining what is being said to them? How is their energy? If they had a choice, what do you think they would like the 45 minutes of your talk to be like?

Often when I go to an engagement, I go up to people before my talk. I always get there early. I make sure all the details are done from a technical standpoint and make sure the person introducing me is going to create the energy I want. Then I turn around and I get to know people, I talk to them, I introduce myself, I see where they're at. Inside my head I have this mega file of information that I can use, but I do not ever plan a talk until I have a chance to listen to the people. Now that doesn't mean they're always talking. Sometimes I just have to look. I have to listen with my heart, and experience as a fellow human being. Sometimes in the middle of an engagement, I have to change directions because I'm not giving them what they need – I can hear that.

Which is a very different approach than most people take.

I will say this – this is an ego thing and I will admit that – but this is a solid thing I can tell you: I am absolutely unparalleled as a speaker coach. I do not know anyone that's a better coach for speakers than I am – it does not mean they are not there, but I've never met them. I am absolutely an unparalleled speaker coach. It is a real gift that I have that's a combination of almost everything that I believe in and I do, I really am. If a person really wants to be good at speaking and they're willing to break paradigms, they can make a lot of money. Of all the things I do and all the talents people have, that's my magic. I can draw that teacher, that speaker, that transformer out of people who are willing.

Where do you think you get that gift from – did you have parents who were good speakers or brothers who were good speakers? Or is it just something that came to you naturally?

Oh gosh no, I've been working on this since I was 20 years old. I'm 52. I've worked every day. I've never stopped learning. I always desire to be better than I was before. I consider coaching and speaking and doing seminars as needing the same basic skill (if you're really a coach and not a counsellor). Just today I was doing something, I was doing a short inspiration on film for something that we're doing and I thought to myself, 'Whoa girl, you need to start doing that again. You haven't been doing that lately.' I think I'm a great speaker because I'm really a great learner and have a great passion for learning.

Do you think that learning is an important part of being an entrepreneur?

Without it, you don't belong as an entrepreneur or a speaker, either one. If you don't love learning, then go back to a job that's 9 to 5 and enjoy it. There's nothing wrong with a 9 to 5 job, I think it's wonderful. But enjoy your life, just have a good time. You don't have to live in an eight-bedroom home or have a 4,500 square foot home. You can live in a small, little two-bedroom home with five kids like my grandparents did and have a beautiful life. If you don't want to continue learning, then let it be okay that you want to have that kind of life. I think that's great.

When you mentioned learning, a lot of people will think 'school'. What was your experience at school?

I was in trouble an awful lot. I was fairly intelligent, but I thought I was pretty stupid. Sports were big for me in school. But, I love to learn and my mother was big on that. I think parents have a lot to do with instilling a love for learning in their children. You don't have to be a genius to love to learn. I think I got it pretty young because my mother was always real creative and she always did some creative things. I remember she used to take us to the library when she didn't have a babysitter. She'd leave us at the library, but before she left she'd sketch out the United States for me and have me name all the states and their capitals. She sketch out Europe for my brothers (my brothers were older) and have them name all the rivers. She always had us doing things, like making up Jeopardy games and stuff like that. My mother was very imaginative and I think the imagination is the key to being a great learner.

Tell me a little bit about *Life Retold*, your latest book.

Life Retold is a book people have been asking from me for 25 years. I finally sat down and wrote it thinking it was pretty much for the people I love, my beloved and my friends and the people that I've worked with over the years. It was pretty much for them. But the response on it has been heart-warming to me and pretty surprising. The book itself is stories and the stories are true-life stories. Yes, they are from my life, and the reason they are from my life is because in the way that I tell the stories I just don't hold back all the icky, negative and shadow stuff of me. In the process of the stories, what I'm hearing back is people are really getting a sense of being okay with who they are, forgiveness is happening for people. I get letters from people that say things like, "The story about your dad, I read it every night before I go to bed and I've done it for like four months. It has completely allowed me to accept my father for who he was for the first time in my life."

The book itself, it's getting really great reviews, it's doing very well and people just enjoy it. Plus it's a book that's easy because you read a story, put it down, and read a different one the next time, which is pretty fast. It's not a complicated book; it's a simple book. I think what it's giving people is a sense of inner acceptance and the freedom that comes with that.

\

More information at: www.liferetold.com
or www.NationalSpeakersClub.com

Linda Franklin

Linda Franklin was the first Canadian woman to own a seat on the New York Stock Exchange. Without a college degree, she went on to manage the trading department for a leading Wall Street investment firm. Her 22-year dream career ended when she entered a transitional period she calls her 'tsunami of change'. Now Linda is a writer and a speaker running her own company, The Real Cougar Woman. She is focused on serving the ever-changing needs of strong, confident, smart women proud to be over 40.

Q. Tell me a little about yourself.

I was on Wall Street for over 22 years and it really was a very interesting time and a great time of learning, because basically I ended up running a trading department where I was in charge of the MBAs and I had never gone to college. On Wall Street, you usually don't even get in the front door unless you have had a college degree. So I did the next best thing – I back doored it.

I began my career as a secretary because I believed that's as high as I could go because I didn't have that college education. If that's what people have always told you, pretty soon you start to believe it. Your own psyche holds you back. But finally I got to the point where I realized as a secretary I was at the top of the ladder with no upside potential. I really wanted to work in the company's trading department, because now I would be on the bottom rung with lots of possibilities.

In those early days I was dabbling into self-help which was just getting its start. I began to really look at who I was and feel my own power for the first time in my life. When I started to believe that I could consciously create what I wanted, it just changed my life completely.

Was there a turning point that changed the way that you thought? Was it something in your personal life or something in your work life?

It started out gradually, but then one night it hit full force. It was right before my 29th birthday, I stopped off and I got a few of the meagre self-help books that were available. I went home and I decided that I was going to spend the weekend reading them. As I started to do that, I started to feel a kind of electricity running through my body and I had no idea what it was. It felt like up to this moment in time I was unplugged and now I was connected to the power source. I knew something very powerful was being born.

So you had a sense of possibility?

A sense of possibility that I never ever had before, and that changed everything because when you believe that you can change it changes you. People start to see you differently – so even before I asked for the opportunity to work in the trading room, I had already started to pave the way for that to happen.

One day I just gathered up my gumption, and I went in to talk to my boss. I told him I wanted to work in the trading department. He looked up at me from his glasses and he said: "I'll give you the chance, but if you don't make it I'm going to fire you because in this firm we don't go backwards." That was a scary decision for me but I said: "I am going to take on that challenge." I started as a clerk, putting in buy and sell tickets and answering phone. At the end of the day, I created our profit and loss statement manually. That was in the late 70s before it was all computer generated.

Within a year of starting that new job I got the surprise of my life. My boss made me a small partner in the firm. I was the first woman to ever become a partner in this all-male company. Even though it was a small percentage – it made a world of difference to me. It helped validate what I was capable of doing.

Yes, wonderful.

Right, so after that everything progressed. The next thing was, I started to actually trade. My boss made me choose five stocks to trade for real. I had been doing it in my head all along, but now he wanted to track my performance. I was scared to death. So it was with these five stocks, I learned to trade. He watched me, mentored me, he said: "I don't care if you make money – this is more about learning the technique. This will show me what you are really made of."

So we did that for a while and it proved that I was good. I had a real talent for trading. The five stocks grew into hundreds and into multi million dollars. I don't remember how many years passed before a new opportunity presented itself.

In addition to running our own trading department, we were also specialists on the floor of the New York Stock Exchange. My boss decided he wanted me to go to the floor and further hone my trading skills. And, that's how I got my seat. I was at our post trading securities with hundreds of floor brokers. They had to come to me when they wanted to buy or sell the securities that I was the specialist in. I did that for a year before returning to run my own trading department.

It took only two years after that to become head of the department.

There weren't many women working in those days. How did you find that?

In our firm, there were no women – just the secretary and the bookkeeper, that was it. Down on the floor, there just a handful. But that was okay because I loved working with men.

I love working with men because they are less sensitive than women. All that testosterone brought out my male energy and that was good for the job I was doing. I did manage to maintain my feminine side as well. That's really important to remember – we are women. In my entire career I never ever had a problem with sexual harassment, even down on the floor, because I always set boundaries. If anybody crossed over those boundaries, I would make it very clear, very quickly that they had. So I really think it's a woman's responsibility to take care of herself and I think that that's an important thing to say for your book. This was a male bastion but they did respect a strong woman that held her ground.

So going back to what you said earlier: you had no college degree, you didn't believe you could do it. Other people might look at you from the outside and say: "Linda is just an exceptional woman. Gee, there's something special about her." Do you think it's possible for *anyone* to achieve what you've achieved?

Yes, I think it's possible for anyone to achieve what I have and hopefully am continuing to do. The most important thing is to believe in yourself, because if you have any doubt and fear, you're going to end up sabotaging yourself. I'm not saying that every day is a perfect day and that you don't have those doubts and fears but you can't dwell on them because it really, really does hold you back. It takes you into a downward spiral. Always, the most important person to you is you. And it helps to have a mentor.

Who was your mentor and at what stage did you have your mentor?

My mentor was actually the senior partner of the firm that gave me my big break. We had a wonderful relationship throughout my entire time at the firm and he continues to be my friend today. We still go out to lunch. He not only taught me everything that I needed to know about the business, he also taught me so much about life and it was wonderful.

You have to be the right mentee to have the right mentor. A lot of people want a mentor but they're not willing to be the right person, and by the right person I mean you have to show them that you're really listening. I was like a sponge and everything he told me I used right away so he could see that I was listening. So many people say they want help, and then they don't take it. When that happens, the mentor loses their enthusiasm for teaching you. So I think that that's very important. Having the right mentor is definitely a gift. You work harder to make them proud.

Yes. So a large part of it is mindset?

In my case, obviously, a large part of it was mindset and a large part of it was having the mentor to guide me because I did not really have the education to set me up. So I learned, as I do with most things in life, through on-the-job experience.

Tell me a little about The Real Cougar Woman. After your 25 years on Wall Street, what made you decide to set up The Real Cougar Woman?

When I left Wall Street, I went through, as you've mentioned my tsunami of change and that was because I was very, very attached to my corporate identity and when I didn't have that any more I was completely lost, completely. I didn't know what to do when I woke up in the morning. All of the beliefs that I had set in place seemed to have fallen by the wayside. So I spent a year wallowing. Then I decided I had to figure out what happened to me because I was still this powerful woman and I somehow had to find her again.

I started my comeback by making a list of all of the things that I needed to find answers to and that included: finding everything I could about menopause because the traditional methods weren't working for me. I went out and I interviewed so many doctors and read hundreds of research reports and ended up with so much important information. I also did a lot of research on fading beauty. I was 48 years old and really needed to find out how to make myself look more youthful and vibrant. I did research on relationships, but the most important thing that I did was really go out and fill up my spiritual reservoir again. I was curious as to why the beliefs that had worked so successfully for so many years started to fail. I was intent on finding out everything that was missing.

I began to study with some of the spiritual leaders whose books I had read and tapes I had listened to. I went to their workshops and their seminars and I started to appreciate what was really important. To form new beliefs – and it is those beliefs that have helped take me to where I am now. The most important thing is to feel good every day. When you are in that feeling good place, you are vibrating in consort with the universe. It's kind of a law of attraction only a lot more.

You mentioned that it was a very difficult year.

Very difficult.

If you take yourself through the emotional states, how did you pull yourself out of that very low emotional state into this higher vibrational frequency where you felt able to move forward?

Well, because I did have a big spiritual backing. Even though I was going through a bad time, I didn't hit rock bottom. I knew what I was doing was destructive, but just couldn't see the light at the end of the tunnel. But finally, I did. Time is a great healer. It's not like one magic day, you wake up and you say everything is back on track; it's kind of a process.

For that tough year after Wall Street, I thought I had lost everything that was important to me. I didn't know whether I would be able to replace it or reinvent myself. It happens to so many people in mid-life – both men and women. I remember when I was going through that time people would ask me: "How does it feel to be retired?" Then the hackles on the back of my neck would go up because the last thing in the world I wanted to be was retired. It was like an embarrassment to me, but I didn't know what my next step would be.

Tell me about some of the people and the clients that you've worked with. How have their lives changed through joining The Real Cougar Women?

Well, The Real Cougar Woman is strong, confident, smart and proud to be over 40. I work with so many women. I get hundreds of e-mails everyday and they want to learn more about what they can do to become everything they can be. Woman over 40 – because of society and the way we've all been kind of brainwashed – think that that is the time in our life when it starts to slow or that we're diminished or that we start to fade into the woodwork or nobody cares what we have to say any more.

While doing research for my Real Cougar blog, I started to read a lot about the traditional definition of a cougar, which was a lonely sad desperate woman on the prowl for young guys. I looked at that and I said: "Oh my God, these aren't the women that I know". So I wanted to take that on, I wanted to debunk that myth and say: "No, that's not who we are at all. We are really absolutely fabulous females".

So all of the women that I talk to now and that are members of my Real Cougar Woman Club are so happy to have this new image to attach to. They feel comfortable about talking about all the things they are going through. It's a great support network.

You've mentioned this tsunami of change – do you think everyone goes through the tsunami of change or do some people skip it and they're too scared to confront it?

No, I don't think you have a choice. I think everybody on the planet goes through a tsunami of change, whether they admit it or not. A tsunami happens just for the reasons that you said, that over the years we do not confront the little problems. We like to sweep them under the rug and then eventually all of these little problems – I call them the small little waves – eventually merge into this one huge tsunami. These waves can actually swamp the boat if you don't know how to handle it. I don't think you just go through one, I mean, I've gone through three and I probably will have more. They emerge at different growth spurts in your life.

What would say the three tsunamis have been for you?

Well the first one is when I was really young and I decided to pick myself up and move to New York, and I did that at 19. Then the second one was at 29, what I was explaining to you when I discovered that I could consciously create my life the way I wanted to. Then the third one, again, was when I left Wall Street. I don't know what the fourth will be, but I can guarantee you it's going to arrive one day.

So if somebody came to you today and wanted to turn their life or their finances around, what advice would you give them?

I would say, first of all, the most important thing is to take responsibility for who you are and what you want to do. It's all about you! When you look in the mirror in the morning, you have to be perfectly honest with what you're doing or not doing with your life. It's very easy to blame others and not take responsibility, but that only makes you a victim. The bottom line is – it's always about you so you have to make a plan. You have to take a look at your life and say: "Okay, what are the things that I like and what are the things that I don't like?" The things that are working for you, hold on to. But you have to be able to let go of the things that aren't working for you. That's very difficult for a lot of people because the fear of the unknown is even more horrifying than the unhappiness of the known. So they really have to let go of that.

You have to sit down and say: "Well, what do I really want to do?" A lot of women have lost themselves and they don't remember what makes them happy. They don't remember what things that they did that really made them feel fabulous. They have to find a way to re-connect back in to what makes them feel good. Ask: do I want a new job? Do I want a new man? Do I want to start my own business? What is going to make me happy?

Why do you think they have lost their way? Do you think it is through societal brainwashing or through programming in childhood?

All of it. I think that women have lost their way because women have always been programmed to take care of other people, whether husband, family, children, friends and then you end up at the bottom of your priority list. After a while if you're always pleasing other people you forget how to please yourself.

You think that applies to women more so than men?

I definitely think it applies to women because that's how women are seen. They're caregivers. The men are the hunters and the gatherers and we're the nurturers and taking care of everybody, but that's changing. The Real Cougar Woman doesn't feel that way.

So you're promoting a very positive image for women and you said you want people to rediscover how powerful they really are. So really, you're tapping into something that's already there?

It's definitely there, you just have to rediscover it. We all have it. I say that every woman has a Real Cougar inside of her just waiting to be unleashed. She just has to give herself permission to do it and she has to stop worrying about what other people are thinking and saying and start to really focus on what she wants – because in the bottom line that's all that counts.

When you are that woman that is really happy with what she's doing, the woman that feels fulfilled, that woman that feels nurtured, then you are able to help the other people around you. You're the best friend. You're the best wife. You're the best lover. You're the best because you are that light. You are that energy. People see that in you. They want to be like you. You never want to allow anyone to drag you down. You want to bring them up to where you are.

So you need to let go of the past. You have to have a plan for moving forward. Ideally have a mentor.

Yes and you have to allow yourself some fun time. That's an important part of my "I Create" success formula. Make some time to have fun every day, even if it's only 10 minutes. Whether it's meditation, whether it's listening to a tape, whether it's having your bubble bath, have sex, whatever it is, find that time to let go, take a deep breath and feel who you are and what you want to do.

How do you start your day? What do you do in the first hour of your day – what does that look like?

You know, it's starting to change because I'm really getting to appreciate the spiritual component again. I find that the more I do that, the more things manifest in my life. So I'm waking up every day now and I'm saying: "How may I serve?" and playing my Tibetan singing bowls.

"How may I serve?" So it's not thinking, 'what can I get or what can I do?'

No, it's: "How may I serve? Please help me make me the vehicle that will really resonate with other women. How can I teach them what they need to learn? How can they relate to me?" Because if they can't relate to you, then they are not going to accept you. If they don't trust you, they're not going to accept you. So by asking these questions, I feel I don't have to do it alone. This is my spiritual team helping me.

So I have over this last two years, built a trust with these women. Women are sceptical and they need to trust you before they will spend any money on your products or services.

Also, I believe in education. I've started this new business and I knew nothing about publicity and marketing because that was not in my business background. I had to learn all of that from scratch. If you're going into a new business and you don't really understand everything that entails, you have to find the right people that can help you. It entails finding a mentor, only this time you're probably paying for it. But I think it's really, really important that you do find someone that could really teach you how to make the most of what you've got.

So how important do you think it is to have a team of people helping you?

I think it's very, very important to have a team. Now in Wall Street, in business and corporate life, you always have a team. If women are going out and wanting to start their own business, they don't. It's usually just them. Then they get completely overwhelmed because there's so much work to do and they are working 12, 14, 16 hours a day and they just become completely exhausted. When that happens, the fun, the enjoyment and the good feeling that you had at the beginning very quickly goes away. Not a good thing. You have to set up a team.

So what I have done and I'm advising other women to do is set up a virtual team. You do not need employees that are on your payroll, but you can put together a team of experts that have a specialty and they're called virtual assistants and you find them online. You find them on Facebook. You find them on Twitter.

Ask yourself what you need – a web designer; a web technician; someone to help start a blog; a graphic designer; a printer; a fulfilment house and so on. So some people have as many as 15 or 16 virtual assistants on their team. Now they may not be using all of them at once, but they're there and that allows you to spend your time being the brain trust. Coming up with the next money-making idea. Every idea takes at least 10 steps to implement, and you are the project manager. It's very important to do this because it makes it fun – not drudgery.

So how do you pick the jobs that you give to other people and the jobs that you do yourself?

Well the jobs you give to other people are the jobs you usually don't want to do yourself and the things that you don't feel qualified to do. Like setting up shopping carts on your website. If you're going to sell online, you need some way for people to pay for it. I can't do that so I go out and look for people to do it. You ask for references and pick the best person.

If you had to identify the top three mistakes that entrepreneurs make when they're starting out, what would you say that they would be?

I think that the top one is believing they can do it all themselves. I think the second one is they don't they have a business strategy. And the third, they haven't identified their target market.

Okay, so those are the top three mistakes. So those are the top three things that they need to avoid if they want to succeed?

Right and you'll learn by your own mistakes. Believe me, I'm not a genius, I've made all of these mistakes but hopefully you get smarter as you go along. Again, I'm getting the education from people that I respect that have done it. I can actually see their progress and because they have done it they can teach me.

So continuing education, again, is really important?

Well, continuing education yes – not necessarily a college education. When you're an entrepreneur, you want to follow entrepreneurs that are actually doing similar things that you're doing. You want to monitor their growth so you can be following their model when it's working. It's not just book learning. I think that that's very important and I'm choosing my coaches very, very carefully.

What about somebody who perhaps is in debt, and has got

themselves in a pickle with their business, and they're worried about spending more money on getting a mentor? What would you say to somebody like that?

Well, it's a very ticklish situation and I hear it all of the time. Getting into debt is certainly never a good thing, but if you really have a business that feels like it's on the verge of breaking through, then you might have to go that extra mile. Spend your dollars carefully and on the person who is most likely going to show you how to take that last important step. Someone who can provide you with a good model to follow. A person who can show you how to charge enough for your services.

Charging enough is a big problem for women. They undervalue themselves. The smart entrepreneurs are making it even in this depressed economy. Their pricing is actually staying where it was. So much is about perception. People believe if they pay more, they're getting more. I would say, don't get yourself in debt where you're not going to be able to put food on the table. But if there's that one person that you really believe is going to help you, take that one extra step.

 So your tips for choosing a mentor – if somebody was choosing a mentor – how would they go about choosing between say two or three?

I think you have to choose a mentor or a coach that you can see is giving you the best results and it's not just because they're telling you that they are. Look at them. Everybody has got websites. Everybody has got a lot of things that they're doing. Which ones do you feel are the most successful and the ones that you can learn the most from, and the ones that are not teaching you only theory but practical ways to really get your business booming? How do you make money? A lot of them are very, very big on theory but I like the ones that are saying: "Okay, by the end of this course, you are going to have your first product or your second product or your third product ready to go, because I'm going to give you the step-by-step of how to make it profitable for you."

So a lot of it is about goal setting. Setting goals, then working towards them and breaking it down to small bite-size chunks.

Yes but the bite-size chunks are chunks that you're not doing all by yourself. As I said before, you need a team because you have to keep several balls up in the air at the same time and you can't do it by yourself.

Being an entrepreneur is tough. There are so many different components. But that's a whole other discussion.

One of the things that's great about having your own business or working for yourself is if you do have a family to look after, it's much easier than working for somebody else. Having to pick up kids from school, dash around and try to squeeze everything in because of course, you're much more in control of your own time...

Yes you are, and a lot of women say that. They can be there for their kids or pick up their kids or whatever, and then they can be writing or doing what they need to do at midnight. But I said this before: women want to be all things to all people and you just can't. That's when you start to lose your identity and lose your joy because you're so tired and so overwhelmed all the time, so everything including your business suffers.

But yes, working for yourself does give you more flexibility. I mean everything is a give and take. You don't have a defined income coming in every week and a lot of times you do not have the benefits that you have when you're out working, like health insurance. Yes, your time is a little freer, but you always give up something to get something. There are never any free lunches. I think you learn that very quickly.

So tell me a little about your own plans for the next few years. What does the future hold for you?

What I see for The Real Cougar Woman is growth. I see a really big community. I see a movement. I see The Real Cougar movement. I'd like to see every woman in the world over 40 attaching to this way of being your own woman – of feeling that you're in control of your own life. I see more products. I see seminars. I see retreats. I see speaking. My book *Don't Ever Call Me Ma'am* will be out. I have a million dreams.

If anyone wants to find out more about you and what you do, where would they go?

The website is www.therealcougarwoman.com. I write my blog three or four times a week on relationships, beauty, health, finances and spirituality. They can also subscribe to my by-monthly e-zine which has some great tips, and all the updates on my products and services. They can join The Real Cougar Woman Club which is a great network for women over 40. I have over 1,000 members and it's growing every day. It's a place where your voice can be heard in a community of woman who really understand you.

How does the media react to The Real Cougar Woman?

I'm like a little media darling right now. The media is attached to the older woman out looking for younger guys. When they interview me, I say: "No. That's not who she is. If a woman over 40 is choosing to be with a young guy, I think that's fabulous, but she's not out chasing him. He's actually out chasing her because she has so much to offer."

So every time I go on these shows, even on the Today Show, I usually get asked the why's about these relationships. Then I turn it around and say it's all about the women. A Real Cougar doesn't define herself by the age of the man she chooses to be with. In my book *Don't Ever Call Me Ma'am* – The Real Cougar Handbook For Life After 40 – it's all about how to be that strong, confident, independent woman.

You've had an amazing career. If you had to pick out one high point – and it must be very difficult – but if you had to pick out a real high point of your career, what would you say it was or is?

I think it's yet to come – but up until now I would have to say the opportunity of running my trading department on Wall Street and now The Real Cougar Woman. I'm starting to feel that I'm really touching the lives of these women and that's like, Oh My God. Some of the stories, they're just unbelievable and they melt my heart. I guess Wall Street was a high point in my masculine energy and The Real Cougar Woman is the high point in my feminine energy.

I'm going to share the stories in the new book. I have lots of stories in there. I have asked them to write me with their stories and they have. Yes, they are going to be part of the book. I think stories are a wonderful way to get a message across.

More information at: www.realcougarwoman.com

TEN

Lynne Franks

Lynne Franks is a businesswoman, an author, a broadcaster and a speaker. She founded her first public relations company at her kitchen table when she was just 21 and it went on to become one of the most well-known PR agencies in the world. She's said to have been the inspiration for the UK's television sit-com 'Absolutely Fabulous'.

Q: Lynne, tell me a little about your childhood. Did you always think you'd be as successful as you are today?

Did I ever think I was going to be successful? No, I don't think anyone thinks as a child that: I want to grow up and be a success in what I want to do. If you're a particularly sensitive, focused child, maybe. But I certainly wasn't focused. I wanted to grow up and do something I loved and enjoyed, I suppose, if anything. Not that I knew what that was – not that I still know what that is actually.

From that perspective, yes, I've always loved working with people and writing, speaking, organising things. So I suppose in a way, whatever I enjoyed as a child I've managed to make a part of my career. Actually, that's one of the things that I teach with my programmes. I teach women to look back to their childhood or their teenage years, and remember the things that they loved to do, and how they can bring that into their professional life.

Do you think women find it easy to access that childhood joy?

Yes, I do. I think women find it easy to connect with their true self, because traditionally they have not had to wear as many masks as men. Having said that, that's not strictly speaking quite so true any more because women have gone into the men's business world and started thinking they have to act and talk and be like men. Then they have to get back in touch with themselves. So it depends really. I think when women have children themselves, that's when they're able to access their inner child again – then, it's quite easy for them.

You left school at 16 and started work as a typist – what led you to set up your own PR business?

Well, in between starting as a shorthand typist and starting my own business, I became a journalist. I worked for a couple of years on the first teenage girls' magazine in the country with people like Eve Pollard and Janet Street-Porter. I was very young when I started writing. I always want to be a journalist anyway. Then, I went to work at Freemans Mail Order Company, writing magazines there, and I couldn't then get the job I wanted back in the media. There weren't that many jobs around for young journalists in those days, young women journalists.

So I went into PR by default and found that I had a natural knack for it. I started working with some very talented young fashion designers, specifically Katherine Hamnett, who's been a friend and client for about 20 years. I realised that if I couldn't get the journalist job I wanted, PR made a very good second – and in fact, I ultimately came to view it as a very good first.

Was it easy in those early years setting up your business?

It kind of was, which is remarkable really when I think that we didn't have mobile phones, we didn't have computers, we didn't have easy communication systems. It amazes me how we ever got anything done really, when I look at how much we rely on it now. But I was sharing a flat with my boyfriend, I had one client paying me £20 a month – that was Katherine – I had an answer phone. I had a Saturday job, that's what I did. I worked in a shop on Saturdays, as a secretary, and that's how I earned the money to keep myself.

I used to have this old car and I used to fill the car up with fashion samples. Soon enough, I had another couple of clients. We'd go off to Fleet Street, we'd go around IPC Magazines, and show my clients' goods and persuade the journalists that they were worth featuring. It really did take an awful lot of balls to do what I did – but when you're 21 years old, you're full of enthusiasm and believing in what you do. I just did it and I taught myself. I had worked in a PR company at one point as a secretary for about a year, so I knew how to structure a press release and I knew how the system worked. But that was very 'old school' PR. This was about very long boozy lunches by ex-army guys who would then commission some young woman to write a piece about it.

So was it just a matter of trial and error?

Yes. I started my own PR agency, it was probably in about 1970. There really weren't any mentors. Audrey Slaughter was a woman's magazine editor who'd been my boss at Petticoat. So she'd been a mentor for me then – but as a PR, it really was the beginning of a new career, a beginning of a new industry. It was very, very different so I really taught myself. There were a number of young women that were starting little agencies, especially in the fashion industry. I wasn't on my own, but there was nobody doing it quite the way I was. I then went far broader than fashion quite early on, and that was quite unique.

So how did you learn – through reading books?

No, I didn't read any books. It was trial and error really. Just trial and error and understanding the psychology of influence.

Lynne Franks PR grew to a global brand in just 10 years. During that time, you advised many of the world's top retailers and designers. What made the company so successful? What made it stand out from all the others?

Creativity I think – creativity, passion, energy. Getting out of my comfort zone, always pushing the boundaries, not even *seeing* the boundaries actually. I had a few designers who were upset because I didn't have anywhere to have catwalk shows. So I decided to put a big tent up. I went all over London looking for a venue. I found somewhere originally in Kensington then we moved to Chelsea, raised all the funds to do it, and created London Fashion Week. It was like there were no boundaries or barriers. If I thought of the ideas and I thought they could work, I'd make them happen. When I look back at that young Lynne, I really applaud her because I'd be much more cautious now and also a little bit more cynical. But back then it was: "Hurry up! Come on, let's do it" and I'd do it.

You've been described as a lifestyle guru and a visionary. As you mentioned, you launched London Fashion Week. You brought Swatch watches and designer jeans to the attention of the British public. How do you spot the next big trend?

I don't even think about it. It's like I have a highly-tuned radar to sort of sniff out lifestyles and plug into the Zeitgeist. I've always had it even as a child at school. I've had school friends say: "Don't you remember you were always the one that was saying this was the latest music and this was the latest frock." So even now, even at my advanced years, I still know what's going to happen before it happens. I think I've just got very popular taste, so I kind of work out what I enjoy doing. It always amazes me when I suddenly see that I'm not alone. But I always seem to be just slightly ahead of the crowd and it's enjoyable. It's great fun to do it that way.

These days, people are bombarded with all sorts of advertising and PR messages. Can you define what was so different and unique about your campaigns?

Well they really did bring together multimedia in a way that hadn't been used before. When I say multimedia, again, in those days we didn't have social networking. We didn't have all the different technological breakthroughs that are there now, but we did have live events. We did have print media, we did have television and we did have broadcast media.

So if I was going to create an event or some kind of promotion as I did for Brylcreem let's say… Let's use that as an example. Brylcreem would've been very popular in the 40s. Suddenly, the advertising agency thought this would be fun for young boys and then it was up to me to convince the young boys. So we did something called The Brylcreem Boy. We went all over the country looking for, I think it was 'BRYL' and BRYL was an acronym for something. I can't remember what it was now – 'brilliant', 'real', 'young', 'original' or something. So we'd go to shopping centres and we had little booths outside Boots. So Boots was thrilled and they were the biggest retailer. These boys would come and get interviewed and filmed. Then we'd take the finalists and put on an event in the local disco. This was in the 70s or early 80s, and it was a very interesting way of doing it at that time.

We'd tie up with a trendy magazine like *ID* or *The Face*. Then we'd have these guys come on to a sort of a male fashion show, Miss World type of thing, but done in taste. Then we'd vote the winners and have a semi-final, featured in the local press. Then we'd take it down to London and get it on the national press. We had a very trendy little magazine that we produced that we'd give out everywhere, about what was also bright, real and original at that time. That included what would be the right beer to drink and the right clubs to go to. We did it all over the country.

It wasn't really PR. I mean we called it 'PR' because there wasn't really a name for it. I'm not sure there's a name for it now really. It was viral marketing and all kinds of below-the-line stuff. When I think about it, what we could have done if we'd had YouTube, Facebook, Twitter, and all the other toys, oh my God! But we did pretty well, I have to say. We did phenomenally well. Again, it was thinking 'out of the box' all the time. No other agency, still even now, has got that kind of understanding of "let's hit every single area we can".

In some ways, I do feel sad that I sold the business. In some ways I'm still dying to do all that stuff again, but then I'm so involved with other things that you can only do so much. It wasn't my idea to sell the business; it was my ex-husband's. I would've kept going for sure because it was such fun. I had such fun doing it.

So it was fun. It was your passion.

Well, I'm not passionate about the products in the same way. I'm passionate about human rights, women's rights and the environment. That's what I'm passionate about, but it was just incredibly good creative fun. It was very creatively fulfilling. Also, I'd be working in a team with bright young people who I adored. At that point in my life, I was exactly where I should have been – which was leading a team of great creatives into blue sky with thinking that just broke down any previous predetermination of what PR was all about.

As I'm talking to you now I realise it hasn't been done since either – not in the same way we did it. When I've had reunions or bump into members of my team, they all say, "God, you think we did this and we did that." Brylcreem, I just plucked that out of the air. But I can give you dozens of examples and we just had over 20 years of it. We had extraordinary things going on.

Is it possible to do PR without spending a lot of money?

Again, it's defining what PR is. If you're really trying to get over your message and influence your customer, whether that's a B2B customer or the consumer. So can you do it yourself? Well I think today with the Internet you can, if you're really savvy about how to use it. Can you get things written about you in the newspapers, even if you have no money? If you're smart, you can, if you've got a great story.

Let's take an example. A young woman who was previously the manager of Woolworths... and she re-launched it as Wellworths in Doncaster and it's been this enormous success. Somehow, she told somebody and somehow it got to Chris Evans on Radio 2, then he got behind it and that brought in all the national press. If you saw the programme on the BBC about her, she was not a natural PR woman. She was very self-effacing and shy, but it just happened organically. I mean look at the Susan Boyle phenomena. It was on national television, but some things can happen organically when it's a story in itself.

I was going to say it's a lot tougher. But actually I think it's probably a lot easier – though there's a lot more competition around. If you think of how many small business owners there are – small to medium size, particularly women – all trying to get their products out there and fighting for space, you've got to be very, very smart.

When people think of PR, they tend to think of gimmicks. You tried to do something different didn't you? You tried to do something ethical, with less gimmicks?

It depends how you define 'gimmicks' really. I would always try to do it in an ethical way. But I think the difference was that you can be ethical, but you can also be creative. So I wouldn't choose to use the word 'gimmicks', because gimmicks can cost you huge amounts of money. I can think of when one soft drink company re-launched with a blue can, it might have been Pepsi. The PR Company hired Concorde, painted it blue and flew it over London. That's an expensive way to get PR. I've never thought, 'spend the most money'. I've always thought, 'let's be the most creative.'

You eventually decided to sell your business 10 years after founding it. In your biography, you described this as a 'life and death' decision. What led you to sell it off?

My two best friends were PRs and they died of cancer within a couple of years. That's the really big thing that got to me. But really, I had to sell because my ex-husband put pressure on me. He wanted out, he was my partner in the business and he wanted the money. At that time I was very exhausted and what I really should've been told was: "go and take a sabbatical for few months". Also, what seemed like a huge amount of money at the time was very tempting, but the reality is that nothing lasts forever, including huge amounts of money.

So I was concerned when my two best friends died. It gave me a real shock to my system, as if to say: "Do I really want to continue doing this?" It all happened at the same time. It was like loads of offers came in. My husband wasn't as attached to this as I was. He wanted out and wanted make a lot of money and I was just exhausted. So I think that's how it was.

Now looking back, 15 years on, I feel I just needed a really good rest.

I'd brought up two children. I'd tried to be the perfect mother, perfect wife, perfect businesswoman and it was just too much pressure. I think we women do put ourselves under huge amounts of pressure, and there has to be a way of doing it in a different way, and that's what I'm constantly looking at. I look at some of those very, very successful women entrepreneurs currently out there making millions. They work very, very hard. They are all juggling families and I think it is a question of us saying: "what are our values, how do we want to live and is that making us happy?" Having our children brought up by nannies isn't always the answer. I certainly had to rely on that. I think women are still going through a lot of self-discovery about what makes them happy.

So what did you do in the years that followed?

The years of the wilderness. I went on a journey of self-discovery, truly. I went to live in different places, visited different teachers. I became a bit of a workshop junkie. I spent time with my kids, started writing. After a few years, I went to live in the States and started another PR business over there. I wrote *SEED* which I had always seen as an opening to a whole business, philosophy, products based on this whole concept of 'a feminine way to do business' which for me was a kind of answer to what we're talking about. In other words: can women create some kind of economic independence, creative fulfilment and still be true to themselves?

So this is a question I've been asking myself for a long time and which I now teach to other women. I think it comes back to that very first question you asked me, which is: "What is success?" Is it being the biggest, or the richest, or having the most cars? I've been there. I had the biggest house on the block. I had support staff. I had a driver and a chauffeur and a beautiful expensive car and first class travel everywhere. So being the generation I am, I kind of experienced all that, and then I went, "actually, who am *I* in all this?"

So it's really an inward look and reflection – which we don't do enough because we get caught in the *doing* and not the *being*. Who am I and what is it I really want to do in my life? What are my values and what does 'success' mean to me? So that's why now I teach workshops on that very thing.

So stillness?

Stillness is something I never had when I was running a business. It's something that I certainly have now. I meditate regularly and I walk the dog, sit in the garden, try and turn off my Blackberry and, yes, try to find that stillness.

You're a passionate advocate of women's enterprise. Tell me about your book *The SEED Handbook: The Feminine Way To Create Business*.

This bubbled in my consciousness for some time and as I've said, I wrote it in the States. I'd had the idea for some time. I also reconnected with Ann Field, who was a friend from England who's a brilliant illustrator who was living in L.A. So we both lived in LA. I went off and wrote it in about three months or less, staying at my then boyfriend's little farm in the middle of the Californian countryside. It really resonated for me. I got some great publishers involved and I brought it out simultaneously all over the English-speaking world.

So I put everything I'd ever learned from PR and communications into the promotion. I had a big launch at Bloomingdales in New York, and then the same thing over here. I just talked about it every chance I had on any media that I could. At the time, calling something 'the feminine way to do business' or 'the feminine way to create business' was so different. I think it was only 2000. It was only nine years ago. Now it's almost a sentence that's accepted as part of the English psyche. It's embedded now.

Then, I received a lot of cynicism from the media. It was amazing. They'd say: "So what's so different about women?" I'll never forget going on Woman's Hour and being totally set up with: "What's so different about the way women do business to men?" Yet I knew that the language was different. Clearly, women had huge self-confidence issues. We don't take the same risks as men. Whether it's starting your own small business, whether it's working inside a large corporate arena, or whether it's being a community leader, women were only at that point being perceived as successful if they did it the male way.

It really was Mrs. Thatcher time: speak lower, speak slower, dress like a man. The whole of the financial world – the financial services, banking – all the women dressed like men. I used to go and do talks to them and say: "You don't have to wear a black trouser suit every day." Gradually, you saw them wearing red high heels and red lipstick. Now, one very close friend of mine is a leading banker. She's one of the most successful bankers in the country and she's totally feminine, but in those days it was so different.

So I think although *SEED* is promoted as being a book about how to start your own small business, it's also a social statement saying: "it is time now for women to be true to themselves and still be successful on their own terms." We've still got a long way to go, but it's further down the line than it was. That's how *SEED* has developed into women's leadership programmes in large companies, workshops, individual coaching, and all sorts of things.

So tell me about the programmes that you run for women.

The language is very different and they are very much values-based. They open up conversations, whether they're women in corporations, large corporates or SMEs. They look very much at values, the individual values. They're also very focused on ethical practices, barter systems, cooperation, multi-tasking and peer group work. So I've created something, which is SEED Circles. Again, I'd started doing it quite a few years ago – and now there are a variety of support circles out there for women. But women work well in a support group, whether it be a writers' group or whatever it may be. So many of these SEED Circles meet regularly, they support each other and they share what's going on for them and I'm in the process of structuring those in a sharper way.

I've also started a social networking site. The idea of it is for women to promote their businesses and talk about their own events. Every day we get new members, and it's become enormous. We get a lot of women from the States, but mostly from the UK, who just want to network with like-minded women. So that's bubbling away.

What I'm looking at with *SEED* is how we can digitalise the workshops that I do and the coaching programme that we have, the women's start-up programme. I'm really looking at digitalising as much as I can and marketing it in a different way. That's been something I've been working on for quite some time. I don't want to run a big business any more. So how can I make this a smart virtual set-up that gives women whatever it is they need.

What sort of challenges do women face in business? Do they face different challenges to men?

It really comes back to confidence – all the time. It doesn't matter where they are, it's actually about self-confidence. That is something men don't seem to have a problem with in the same way. I'm not saying all men are confident, and naturally men have got their issues too. But women are far more likely to hold themselves back because at a very deep level they don't feel that they deserve it. They're coming out of 2,000 years of patriarchal society and the language we have been using is 'chair*man*', 'work*man*', etc.

So we just have to work a different way. It's a *cooperative* way between men and women, but using the strengths of men and the strengths of women. We were talking about feminism earlier and where that went wrong. It really is about women not having to feel they have to be like men to be successful, but they can be women using their own strengths. The professional qualities of men and women complement each other. So it's just like we've got to create a new way of doing things.

So my commitment is to help take that through. My commitment is not about making huge amounts of money or running big businesses, it's about living my life according to my values. I now spend a little of my time working on awareness campaigns, things that I don't earn any money from. My commitment right now is for the terrible situation for women and girls in the Congo and the DRC. So I'm pouring my time into that and I'm totally committed to that.

My plan for my life – which probably comes under your last question ✳ – is for one-third of my life spent for myself, my loved ones, having fun. A third of my time doing things that I don't get paid for but I really believe in, particularly women's rights and sexual violence and things that I really think need a lot of attention right now. And a third of my time doing things that I believe in, that I will get an income from. So at this point, I think that's a pretty good balance.

A lot of businesses are struggling right now – what are the top mistakes that entrepreneurs make when they're starting out?

I think that with this market the way it is, whatever it is that you're making or selling or buying, you've got to stay very aware and flexible. The irony is you have to do a business plan if you're getting investment from your bank. But the fact is that all business plans need to be kept very flexible because we don't know what's going to happen. It's a very volatile world.

Women are proved to be much more cautious than men and that's quite often why they don't do as well as men. So I think it's about getting the balance right. Not being over-cautious, but not extending too early. From research it's shown that men tend to take far too many risks – sometimes rightly, sometimes wrongly. Women tend not to take any, which holds them back. So we just have to get a balance.

What about creating a successful brand? Obviously that's what you're very skilled in. Do you think it's about creativity, about having fun? How would you create a strong sense of brand?

It's a competitive marketplace and to create a brand these days without huge investment is very, very hard. But it can be done and we can see it being done. So I think it's getting the right product, getting the right name, the right logo and the rest of it. You don't see too many from scratch. The number of successful brands that actually make it, compared to the amount that try to make it, are not very many. I think it's always good to look at successful brands that have been done that way. I would quote Ultimo Bras by Michelle Mone, as a perfect example. Model yourself on the successes that you can see out there. The wonderful thing about the Internet, Google, and all the rest, is that you can really research things. So research three or four brands that you admire, that perhaps you're in a similar marketplace, and see how they did it and learn from that.

Why would you single out Ultimo Bras? What was it about that campaign?

It's not just one campaign. It's how she started from scratch. She was a council house girl, with no education and no money. She built her business up to be one of the biggest underwear suppliers in the world. She's only in her 30s now. She's got three or four kids. She's a very good example of somebody who has done it with no help. She didn't go into a family business. She started from absolute scratch. So she is probably one of the best in the world to study right now.

Would you say there was a single turning point that changed your life or has it been a slow series of changes over the years?

I think everybody's life is a series of changing points. I think at any given time you are at a different place in the road where you can go left or right or straight ahead. No, I think there have been many, many times really. The death of my best friends obviously had a huge effect on me. Having my children had a huge effect on me. My grandchildren have had a big effect on me... getting divorced. It's really the personal stuff. It's not like something happened in business and I thought, 'Geronimo, that's it!' It's really all the personal stuff because it changes you as person, it changes your outlook, and it changes your values. I've learned so much from *SEED* by working with other women. I'm supposed to be there passing on my experience, which I can and do. But I've also learned so much. I've worked with thousands of women all over the world. I have been so inspired, and so encouraged, to see what women can do. Every time I teach a workshop, it affects me and deepens my understanding.

What inspires you? What motivates you in your day-to-day work now?

To be a change-maker really – creating change, helping others, being creative. I still love the creative fulfilment in the work I'm doing now. I'm so fascinated by what can be done on the Internet and what is going to be done and how we're going to be communicating together. It's very interesting now if one looks at the success of Facebook and Twitter. Everybody is trying to use Twitter to sell through. For me, it doesn't work. It's just a load of nonsense. Whereas I think Facebook really serves a big social purpose and it is extraordinary how Facebook has become a catalyst for changing people's opinions. I'm still fascinated by all of it.

Do you have any daily rituals? You say you meditate and take your dog for a walk. Do you have any other rituals?

I absolutely love affirmation cards. So I have bowls of angel cards and affirmation cards all over the place. I'm always turning them over to read the messages. I light candles. I like to surround myself with fresh flowers and light candles as part of my SEED manifesto. Usually before a meeting, we will light a candle and play some kind of relaxing music before we start. That's more of a group activity rather than my daily ritual. I like having hot tubs and baths. I like being immersed in water as much as I can.

Over the years, what's the single most important thing you've learned that's accelerated your success?

Always staying true to myself – for right or wrong.

You appeared on the TV reality show 'I'm A Celebrity, Get Me Out Of Here' in 2007. You had to undertake various challenges while living in the jungle with a group of other celebrities. What was that experience like?

I love being outside and I like the outdoor life – that's why I was open to doing it. I got on with most of the people extremely well. Some of the people I disliked intensely, and I found that really hard. Being stuck in a small space, not being able to move, surrounded by flies, was really quite horrible.

I think I've learned a lot from it in retrospect. It's taught me a lot about society. I live and work in the modern world. Reality TV *is* the modern world. So to be able to participate in reality TV on the inside and have that experience was amazing. I don't regret it for a minute, but it definitely wasn't the most wonderful moment in my life for that three weeks or whatever it was.

It was three weeks was it?

It was two weeks inside and a week afterwards with all those people in a hotel. That was just as much like being in a prison as it was in the jungle.

What would you say you learned from it?

I don't think I got cleverer. I don't think I got any wisdom from it. Even if I did things wrong, it doesn't mean I would do anything differently now. I learned how strong I was. I learned that I could do the most disgusting, horrible tasks, and stay completely focused without falling to pieces. So I got a lot of confidence in myself, in my ability to do things. I'd always had various fears, as we all do, of being in trapped spaces, creepy crawlies, rats and all the rest of it. I found out that when I am actually in those situations, I can handle them with no problem at all.

But I also found out that when I am in a situation with human rats, I'm not very good at it. I'm not very tolerant and I'm not very spiritual, even though I think I am. My tolerance level is not very strong at all because I've always been with people I've liked or not spent time with people I don't like, I haven't had to experience that. I also found out that people – just because I always feel like I have to tell the truth – a lot of other people can be very devious. I've not had that experience before. So that was a bit of a new understanding.

Would you do it again?

Yes, definitely… Well, it depends. I would never do 'Big Brother'. I would never do 'Hells Kitchen'. I won't go back in the jungle because they don't take you back, but I would do TV again if it was the right TV show for sure. I like it. I did 'Celebrity Come Dine With Me'. I'm not conscious of cameras. Cameras don't worry me. We were surrounded by cameras and mic's 24 hours a day and I couldn't have cared. That's the problem you see. I don't see it, so then I forget that I'm on camera.

You say that you've reinvented yourself several times already. What are your plans for the future?

I've got about four choices at the moment and I'm really interested to see how they pan out. I think I said earlier about the third, the third and the third. I definitely want to do more writing. I've got these books burning inside me and I want to write them. I want to settle down and not be having all these different homes that I have, and I'd actually like to be in one home and be more grounded. But on the other hand, I suspect that life is always going to be fairly active for me. So I'm very torn between wanting to be this sort of country grandmother and cooking lovely meals and being there for my grandchildren, writing, with a lovely partner. Then, there's another side of me which knows full well that I'm always going to be this chaotic woman running all over the place, doing half a million things, until I physically can't do it any more. So I'm very torn between those two sides of me: the active side of me and the 'being' side of me.

I do want to extend my work and it *is* extending. At the moment, I'm doing all kinds of interesting things with my work. I'm making it more accessible and available to people with technology. I think I'm going to do some TV. So that's raising its head at the moment in quite an interesting way. We'll see.

Actually, I have got another plan that I have yet to do. This is my last big project. I've got the idea really worked out. I never go into details, but I want to create a cutting edge, incredible internet presence for women where they can tell their stories. It's to give women from all areas of society in all countries the opportunity speak to each other, tell their stories, connect and do what women love to do, and learn from each other.

That's a huge thing that I'm working on. The URL is WELL Women's Web – WELL being an acronym for Women's Education Literacy to

Leadership – and that's my final project before I go to the great big female heaven in the sky. I'd love to see that. Well, whether I do it or other people do it, it doesn't matter. I think at the moment more women than men, for the first time ever, are using the Internet. More women than men are using social networking. It's the first time. As technology becomes more and more accessible, we can be now talking to women in Africa, talking to women in Brazil, talking to women in Eastern Europe. Just telling our stories and supporting each other because that's what I think women need more than men. Men don't need to be constantly in connection the way women do. That doesn't mean to say that we stop doing our live connection, because we need that. We need to touch. We need to see. We need to use our body language, but if we can combine that...

As we build our communities, then technology will take on even more importance in terms of learning from each other's experiences. So that's how I see the future of the world is that we really support our communities and at the same time we have our global community. I would like to feel I'm going to be part of that.

More information at: www.lynnefranks.com

ELEVEN

Lynda Dyer

Lynda Dyer is Director of Mind Power Global Ltd. She is one of 58 world-renowned experts filmed for the motivational film 'The Secret'. Lynda is a trainer of: trainers of NLP (Neuro Linguistic Programming); trainers in health and fitness; and personal development programmes. Her motto is 'Everything Is Possible'. She once disguised herself as a man in order to travel from the USA to England to find her father's family. She overcame a debilitating illness that could have killed her and is now known for her boundless energy.

Q: Tell me a little about yourself. Did you always think you'd be as successful as you are today?

Funnily enough as a child growing up, I began to emulate very successful women. My models were successful women like Evonne Cawley because I was a tennis player. She was the person that I modelled in sport because

I was going to be a tennis player like her. Then I found myself when I started to read books. I was reading books and I always tended to gravitate toward powerful, successful women, just always having a dream to travel the world and help people. I wasn't sure of course what I really wanted to do. But as a kid, I kept telling people I was going to be a missionary. If you think about it, in a lot of ways I am.

Was there a turning point at which you made a final decision? Or do you think it's an ongoing process that you never make a final decision of where you're going – you're continually growing?

I'm continually growing, no two ways about it. I don't think we ever stop learning and if we think we're going to stop learning, then our days should be numbered. I've probably learned more since I've left schools and universities than I did in schools and universities simply though the learnings of the universe: what not to do, how to do it better and how to do it different. I've also learned through teaching the NLP, etc, how I did what I did.

Did you have a mentor or a series of mentors to help you?

As a kid growing up, I think you tend to have what we call a 'model' in NLP. As I said, my model was quite often sportswomen, and women in books that were very powerful. I read the story of how the lady from David Jones started, and I began to think: 'I could do that.' I started reading Danielle Steel books. But I found that I could predict the ending, so I stopped reading them – because if I can predict the ending of something, then it's no longer exciting for me. So I went over to people like Bob Proctor, John Canary, and I started looking at those people who started something years ago and just kept at it, kept at it, kept at it, until it became powerful in its own right and started working for them.

Did you have a supportive environment at home? Were your parents entrepreneurs?

No, not at all. My parents were really hard-workers, very loving people. They had high values around family and so we were always really well cared for, loved, cherished and food was a high priority. It was a big family but I had no sense of how to run my own business, or to do anything like that, because my dad taught us to work hard. He came from war-torn England because he came literally out here through The War and he went from, I think, the English Navy to the Australian Navy. When it was time to go back, he asked them: "Could I go back?" They said, "No," and they positioned him in Canberra. Then from Canberra, he met my mom and he stayed here. But we didn't really know how clever he was until in recent times because he is a beautiful carpenter, singer, dancer. But to look after nine people in a family, his role he thought was to work hard and have more than one job. Consequently, that was brought down through us.

That's a model – the 'working hard' model – that a lot of people grow up with. What would be your advice to other people who have grown up with exactly that model through school, through their parents?

That there's a lot that they can teach us in that ethic of working hard. However, working hard on something you love is very different to just working hard. When you're in love with what you do, it's not work. Quite often people will say to me: "You're a workaholic." I will say: "If what I did was hard work, I'd agree with you." But I love what I do, and in fact sometimes I get a little bit annoyed that I'm tired and have to go to bed. Like today, I've had an amazing day of joining lots of different organisations that I want to belong to, lecturing tonight, now talking with you. I mean that's a magical day and I was living in shorts and a t-shirt most of the day until I went to lecture and I got tidied up. You know what I mean? It's like I loved going and lecturing, I loved sitting here and working through what I was working through in my business. Because I have a goal at the end of the day to have a very global business that can assist people to be more – and so I want to be affiliated with all the people that can help me do that.

Is every day a magical day? What do you do when you wake up and you don't have a magical day?

Okay, I think everyone's going to have a not-so-terribly-good day and I think then we can turn that around and look at that. I remember coming into the office and I couldn't get on to anyone, so I just stopped phoning because at most it would have taken me only so far. It's much more effective. Those days are going to happen. However, why work hard and continue to ring people that aren't going to answer the phone? If you're having that sort of a day, leave the office. That's what I say.

So turn a negative into a positive?

Yes, ring a friend and have lunch with him or go and take yourself out for lunch and have some time out. I'll tell you what – first thing Monday morning, I'll bet you've made all those phone calls and created an amazing difference in an hour and a quarter that would have taken you 10 hours had you persevered on the Friday in that environment. The whole universe works in waves. The law of rhythm dictates that you will have 'up' times and you will have 'down' times. The people at the top of the echelon though, their wave isn't quite so big. They don't have the lows as big and the highs as big. They have a continual slope, if you will, that leads to their success. When they have a low, they actually expect it. In those lows, they go: "Thanks for the learnings. You know, it's time to take some time out."

So everything is for learning and you should basically see all the challenges, any hurdles, as an important time of learning.

Absolutely. I'm either winning or I'm learning. There's no failure.

If somebody came to you today wanting to turn their life or their finances around, what would be the top three changes they could make to succeed?

They need to love themselves first. First and foremost, we need to fall in love with us, so I'd get them to stand in front of a mirror and say: "Would you buy from this person today?" Because if you're not going to buy from yourself, then who else will? If you're not going to buy from yourself, then what is it that you'd like to change about you? As a coach I don't change anybody. I'm adamant about that. However, I will give you all the tools and I will be a hard-ass if I need to or I will be a soft-ass if I need to. I will assist you to make great change, but I won't change you. So what is it that *you* need to do? It could be simply a change of mindset. It could be putting your hand up and saying: "You know what, I've got limiting belief and I've got stuff that I accumulated in my life that I don't know how to get rid of. Can you assist me to do that?"

So, mindset, thinking...

Mindset, absolutely. You falling in love with you because otherwise the Law of Attraction doesn't work, does it? How can the Law of Attraction work if we don't fall in love with us? How can we be sending out that love to others, that joy to others, or that confidence to others? Falling in love with you, learning who you are. Who am I? If I'm only associating myself to the position I have in my company, then what happens when I retire? Who do I become? To be frank with you, a lot of depression that's out there in the world today literally has come from people who could only associate themselves with their work role. I am a CEO. I am the Director of Mind Power Global. I am... Well, you know what? I'm not. I'm Lynda Dyer, first and foremost, and if I don't love me, Lynda Dyer... I took many, many years to learn that. One day about five or six years ago, I just got it. I just went: "Aaah, I've got it!"

Do you have a dream team or a team of people who help you now in your day-to-day business?

We were discussing this in my workshop just tonight. The dream team needs to be a group of people that are *not* you, so when you work as who you are, then you hire the rest. In other words if I'm sitting here doing data entry and I'm a creator, what on earth am I doing data entry for?

If I can suggest this: I drew a 'T-junction' – I drew a line across the page and a line down the middle of that line so I had two sides. On one side, I wrote: what are my activities that I'm doing in the day? Then at the end of each day, I'd come across to the accomplishment side and write down: what did I accomplish from each of those activities towards my goal? Now that's how I worked out *who* I needed in my business.

I'm very efficient, like most women. How many women get up in the morning, look after themselves, get the kids off to school and get their husband off to work? Then they get themselves off to work, and then they work an amazing job. They come home and also teach two classes of aqua fitness on the way home. I could then take the washing off the line, have it ironed and back in your wardrobe that night. I could then go and start my business. On the weekends, I would mow the lawn. I could have the house cleaned. But I got lupus. I got a disease of the immune system that nearly killed me.

Goodness. How did that affect you?

The adrenaline hides everything. But that did not lead me towards my goal. My goal wasn't to get sick. My goal was to teach wellness. So I was actually going against my principles of what I was teaching other people, which is what turned it all around.

In a way, that was what turned it around for you?

Absolutely. I believe the universe gave me lupus early because it knew I had the guts to learn what lupus was, and then to be able to teach people how *not* to go there.

How long would you say that period took in your life, that period of learning?

About 14 years. I had no concept of what a fluttering of the eyelid was and it's a calcium deficiency. I had no concept of what a cramp was, because everyone in the fitness industry said it was salt. It's not salt at all. It's a calcium deficiency.

Your self-conscious mind will continue to give you little kicks to tell you to slow down or change routes or do something. So it will give you a pain in the tummy, it will give you a fluttering of the eyelid, or it will give you something that's saying: "If you don't slow down, I'm going to make you". Or it will give you a little car accident. They're just universal things that come to you to say: "slow down". But when we're running on adrenaline, which is an amazing drug, that can hide all the symptoms.

So the best indicator for people to realise where they're really at is to have a look at their body on their day off. On your day off, are you being a lounge lizard and you just don't function like you usually could? Do you love your work so when you're having your day off, you're still in love with life and giving? How many people are living with a victim? Either they or their partner becomes a victim because they work so hard that there's nothing left for the family or nothing left for the kids? Whoever you are on their day off is your body talking to you, because on that day you don't have adrenaline. On that day, your body is saying: "This is how you *really* feel."

Would you say that's one of the top mistakes that entrepreneurs make – because if you're just starting out in business, you're working

on adrenaline and working 60-hour shifts? Of course, a lot of people get hooked into that.

Absolutely. This goes back to 'I am' again. They think, 'I am the business' because in society, for some reason, we tend to get caught up in who we are at work. I am the CEO. I am the accountant. I am a personal trainer. I am...

When we get caught up in our business, we *are* the business. So we think we have to do that data entry; we have to do the marketing; we have to do the sales; we have to do the bookwork. We have to do, we have to do, we have to do – and we're out of flow most of the time. We're not in flow. We're not working to what we were meant to be. Like I'm a creator, so why don't I just be a creator and hire the people who can manage me? If you're, for example, a creator, you tend to be head-in-the-clouds and you tend to think really quickly. That's what I do. I come up with amazing ideas. Does it mean I'm right? No, it just means I have amazing ideas. Then I hire somebody like my business partner who's a really down-to-earth, person who does detail, detail, detail. He looks at the idea and works out if it's going to work or not.

Once people have actually found out what their strengths are, are there any other changes they can make to help them succeed? Obviously, they've got to overcome limiting beliefs. That's quite important. Anything else?

They need to let go of anger, sadness, fear and guilt. Those four emotions can sometimes be handed down generation after generation. How many people are fearful as a grandparent and they raise a fearful daughter who raises a fearful son or daughter?

For example, the people next door, the mother was scared of the dark. Then the children were told: "When you go to Lynda's place, make sure you hold each other's hand. Make sure." I was 10 metres away. I loved the dark, so I had no concept of what they were going on about.

I remember sitting with my son out on the lawn one night looking up at the stars, saying: "Isn't this magical, this whole darkness thing – not just the visual side, but listen to the sounds?" He won an award for the poem we created that night. I thought, 'how different is that to a woman who's putting the fear of death into their child about something that just hasn't got light in it?' That's a limiting belief: I'm scared of the dark.

So sideways thinking. Thinking outside of the box, and thinking differently to other people. This is interesting because you often hear people say: "I haven't got the money" or "I haven't got the knowledge." But what you're saying is it's actually about attitude.

Absolutely. What is attitude? Think about it. Attitude is what I think, what I feel and how I act equals my attitude. Which means what I think is conscious mind, what I feel is subconscious mind – which is all the stuff you've had since you were born and before – and how I act is my body, how do I act on that. If you put those three together, you have your attitude.

So any time somebody gets a result they don't like, you must ask yourself: "What on earth was I thinking to get that result?" Because everything goes through the subconscious mind. All learning, behaviour and change are a subconscious activity, and so it goes through all your programming. Your values, your beliefs, your meta-programmes, your memories, your experiences, your values, everything you had as a child from naught to seven, seven to 14, 14 to 21, etc, is in the subconscious mind.

That's why we can go to a movie and everybody's got a different opinion about the movie because it went up through your experiences, and then you had to think about it. Then if you got emotionally involved with that thought and it was a negative, you will produce a negative result. It's only at the thought level that you have the choice to say: "I'm going to change the mould here and that's not going to be negative for me from now on."

What you're saying is anyone at absolutely any level in society, whatever they're born into, can change their life. They can take power over their own lives and alter the course of their destiny. Why don't more people do it?

It's outside their comfort zone and it's like a terra barrier. If you look at a terra barrier, it's that step that you take that's so different from what you're used to.

What do *you* do if you want to get people outside their comfort zone?

First of all, they've got to put their hand up and say: "I'm willing to change today." I know a lady that's been working in five different real estates, and still to this day blames real estate for her lack of success. You see, there's somebody at what we call the 'effect'. So she's never 'at cause' for her world: everybody in the world will have to go to the psychiatrist in order for her to get better. Because the world is 'at cause' for her state. Now if you are living at 'effect' – in other words you're blaming everybody for where you are – you will never be in control of you. Ever. If you are 'at cause', that means you can put your hand up every part of every day and say: "You know what? I'm at cause for that. I'm at cause for my attitude changing. I'm at cause for this negative tone I've got. I'm at cause for this positive tone I've got."

So have you always worked for yourself Lynda? Or did you start out working for somebody else at the beginning?

No, I started out working for somebody else. I only had the courage to work for myself in about October 1983. So I worked for somebody else for many, many years and I created millions of dollars for a lot of other people. I walked out one day and I said: "The next million I make is going to be mine."

What was the turning point then? Was that your illness at that time that made you decide to do that?

No, quite the contrary. I created an activities program. I had a fetish for opening up institutions so because I missed out on going to university here in Australia by two marks, I worked four jobs and put myself through university as a mature-age student and ended up with two degrees. I always was going to go to university, and I believe everything's meant to be so I needed to grow and grow up, I think. Then after doing that, I've got a lot of stories where I dressed up as a man and went to England to find my dad's family. From the university I was at in Oregon, I hitchhiked across the Canadian Rockies. I have so many stories of setting a goal and making it happen.

You dressed up as a man?

I dressed up as a man to go to England. A man on the campus had a ticket to go to England that he wasn't using, so he said he'd give me the ticket if I gave him my job. It didn't dawn on me until I had his ticket in one hand and my passport in the other that they were very different names. So I decided to be a man when I showed his ticket. In those days, you didn't have to show the two of them together. I realised 22 times they asked me for either my passport *or* the ticket. At no time did they ask for them together until I got to England. Then they put them down on the table, asked me to go to the 'declare' section and I went: "Uh-oh." Then I thought, 'Well, what can they do? They can only send me home.' I just relaxed.

What did they do?

After 20 minutes with this guy, I couldn't stand it any more. Because in my mind, I was making up all the stories that I needed to tell him. I genuinely was finding my dad's family and in the end, I went: "Look-" He said: "You can go through, madam." Then I found my dad's family. It was awesome and the rest is history because he's been back there to reunite with his family. Yes, it's been really lovely.

What did you do after you gave up your job and decided you were going to work for yourself? What was the very first thing you did?

I left because I was in the fitness industry and I was teaching aqua fitness. I left this big hospital programme where I'd set up a million-dollar wellness centre inside a hospital and I already had a reputation for that around the world. I decided that I just wanted to do it for myself, that working for some of these institutions was like working for a brick wall in some respects. In other respects, I loved it because I was opening up the institutions. I was saying that this hospital can be a wellness centre for everyone; it doesn't have to be a sick-house. So I decided that I could do more if I left.

I started teaching aqua fitness and I ran myself ragged. I was teaching so many classes a week, running my business, doing everything myself: teaching, the administration, the marketing, the whole lot. Then an opportunity came for me to teach at the universities and colleges, and I actually turned it down because I didn't think that I was good enough. I didn't think that I could do that, so it was a really interesting phenomenon that I went through.

Then I went from the fitness industry. I created videos and audios. I just knew I had to teach. I started teaching fitness and running seminars. I then developed a programme called *Workshops on Wheels* because I thought it was just ridiculous that people had to come from all over the world or all over Australia to come to me. It was a lot cheaper for me to go to them, so that's how I started travelling. I'd studied fitness. I'd studied health. I was curing myself of a disease so I really knew a lot about the body, and I wanted to teach other people so that they didn't have to go through what I went through.

How did you get your message out there? Was this through direct mail, through publicity material, through the Internet?

I'm just trying to think: at the beginning how did I do it? I'd already had a reputation which was good through working in my job. However to start with, I started with my wall market. I just started to look at some of the health products that were being put out there through multi-level marketing. I researched all that for about nine years, as I said, and I found a company that really moved me. I was getting on very well from their products and so I assimilated my knowledge to the product and then I found an audience obviously that wanted to use that. Then from there, I did that for quite a long time. First of all, I started with the fitness industry and then I started the nutritional side. So then I had both sides. I had the personal training side and the nutrition side so that expanded my business.

Then I realised that without the mindset or the mind, we really didn't have a complete figure here. So I then moved over to the Bob Proctor material, which was also part of the multi-level marketing scene. A lot of the good things around multi-level marketing, or direct selling, are that they get a lot of personal development coaching. I remember going up to this guy and saying: "I'm going to teach this one day." I'd just absolutely found what I wanted to do. He said: "Just get good at multi-level marketing." I said: "No, this is what I want to do." I started really learning the Bob Proctor material. At that time, I had been asked to go and teach in universities. I threw the curriculums in the bin – but don't tell anybody – and I redesigned the whole programme around what I was learning with Bob Proctor.

It was the students, after seven years, who said: "You've got to go and do this full-time." The changes they made were so profound that the teachers at this particular college I was working at were calling me 'the guru'. They said I had way too much knowledge to be teaching at college. The students were taking the information and were really working with it. I had so many examples of kids turning up in classes who had made profound changes because I was working with their personal development.

What motivates you? Has this changed over the years? Say, your motivation 10 years ago, is it exactly the same motivation today or is it different?

It's always been high. People know me as 'energy'. However, I'm more passionate about getting my message out at a global level now than I ever have been. I have a business partner who wants to stay in Australia. It works beautifully because I said to him: "We can still go global and you can still stay in Sydney, because there's this thing called the Internet." He's learning all about the Internet because that suits his profile to do that. It suits me to travel and to see people one-on-one or in big groups. I affect big audiences because people know I care about them. They pick that up straightaway and you're not going to lose that. If you lose that, I think you might as well get off the stage.

You mentioned that when you left your job, you thought, 'The next million I make is going to be mine.' How long did it take you from making that decision?

A very short time. Because once you make the decision, there are four components to making a decision. You've got to decide, and then you must believe. The same thing happened with health. I decided to get well. I believed I was going to get well. I acted on it every day. Third step is act. Last, to expect.

So decide, believe, act, expect.

I decided to go to be that millionaire. I believed I *could* for the first time in my life. I acted on it every day. Was it scary? Absolutely. Then I expected it. So I did exactly what Bob Proctor said to do because he said: "If you don't believe in something, you'll fall for anything." I love that. So I started to believe in me, and what I could do.

I started with the car and I believed I was driving in this car that I wanted. It had to arrive on 11th November. I told the guy at the car shop the whole thing and he said: "Those cars aren't in any more." I said: "Well, the man said they'll be here." He said: "Who's the man?" I said: "Bob Proctor." Anyway, sure enough on 9th November, the car that I wanted came in and he rang me. I said: "I'll be right over to pick it up." I had faith. I absolutely believed. I got the car. Then I got a house that I wanted. I said: "We'll take this," and my husband nearly had a kitten at the time. It was the worst house in the best street, and I just remember banging the wall saying: "That wall's got to go. There's going to be skylight there and skylight there. We're going to add a room there." In my head, I owned it. We moved in. Yes, it was challenging. However I just kept renovating this house over the period of time, and sold it for about four or five times what we paid for it.

Then I thought, 'Well, that was easy. I'll do it with another house.' But I did everything against the grain. Now this is what I'm saying about stepping over that terra barrier. The comfort zone says that you must sell one house in order to buy another house. Well, no, it doesn't have to be that way. That's just what our parents taught us. I actually bought this house and I hadn't even sold the last house. But with faith, I absolutely knew that that house was going to sell. It's just that I didn't want to miss out on this new one by waiting for the other one to sell. I remember my son said: "What did you do today Mom, on Mother's Day?" I said: "I went and bought a house." Then I started to go: "Oh my God, I bought a house!" But I just thought, 'You know what? It's going to work.' I did everything that all the personal development people say. I wrote on the calendar: 'Moving house, 1st October. I just put everything into action. I went for coffee with my Dad and I remember saying to him: "Someone's going to buy my house today. I can see it. There's a family and they want to put in the same sort of energy we put in 20 years ago." I even gave him the price that they were going to pay. I drove home and this family was there with a real estate agent. I was so freaked out by that. I had pictured the whole thing. Isn't that weird?

I had visualised the whole thing. I went to the door. The guy came to the door and I told him how much they were going to offer me. He said: "How did you know that?" I said: "Don't go there!" I sold that house. It was really that easy. With faith, you can do everything. You have one ounce of fear and you've lost your faith. With faith, I moved in here. Everything I ever wanted was in this house: the office at the front, the brick driveway, the huge bedroom, with an en-suite room if I wanted the doggies out in the back, no hallways. There's plenty of room for people to have their own space, as well as joint space, everything I wanted.

Then I thought, 'okay, I've done it here, I'm going to go do it again'. So I went and found an investment property. I remember the real estate lady saying: "You are one gutsy woman." I said: "No, for the first time in my life I just know how to do this and what I want." I was $5,000 short. I had no money. I was $5,000 short and I said to my dad: "You haven't got $5,000, have you?" He said: "No. No, I don't." He rang me back about 24 hours later. He said: "You know what? I've put away $5,000 in a funeral fund." I said: "Well, you're not going anywhere, are you?" He said: "No, I haven't got any plans." I said: "How about you lend it to me and I'll give it back to you with interest?" That's how I bought my investment property.

Then my brother wanted to buy some land and show the world that he could build an environmental estate. I said: "Well, why don't we invest in that?" So all of a sudden, I've got environmental estate land, I've got an investment house, I've got a house, I bought a new car and I'm thinking, 'Gee, that was quick.'

What has been the highpoint over the years?

Believing in myself was a high point because I don't think many people really believe in themselves. I think learning that I can affect so many more people by doing it for me first was probably the biggest change, in that my relationship with my son, my relationship with other people changed profoundly after my relationship with myself changed. Then being confident enough to feel great in your own skin, and take that skin anywhere you like, and be able to assist people to make the changes that they may want to make.

Tell me a little bit about Mind Power Global and what you do in a typical week.

I've now got six businesses actually if you look on my website under lynda-dyer.com. There are six, but Mind Power Global is in essence the mind power. I teach NLP. I teach a Practitioner Certificate, I also teach a Masters Certificate, and I teach those around the world. So I go to China, I do it in Australia, I'll be teaching in the US this year, and I've just had an invitation to come to England and Brussels.

I teach very differently because I teach from a Bob Proctor and NLP perspective. By teaching people, coaching people, they've taught me heaps – what to do, what not to do. I then coach. I do individual coaching. Business coaching to me is individual coaching at the end of the day. All you're doing in business is putting your self-image into your business so you cannot outperform your self-image. Therefore your business is absolutely a replica of who you are. It can't be anything else. When you change, when you think you can affect people more globally – if that's what you want to do – then you will. Because suddenly you realise that you can. If you think small and your business is going to be small, then it will be small. Does that make sense?

Yes, absolutely…

So if we don't feel good about us, or if we think everything has to be perfect, we will take that into our business. If we believe, 'I don't deserve it' then we will not have the money flowing in for our business, because we still feel we don't deserve it. By having coaching at a business level, I coach personally and *then* give a business structure after you're cleared. The business structure is now going to work a whole lot more effectively than if you'd just gone ahead and you still had all your anger, sadness, fear, guilt, limiting beliefs, all the events that you hadn't let go of, and all the people that you hadn't said goodbye to. If they're still in you and I'm just giving you a different business structure, what's going to change?

You mentioned self-doubt, which everyone is hindered by at some point.

You know, if you look at the first five years of your life, you only had a subconscious mind. You didn't have the thought process that is consciousness. So you don't have that ability in you for those five years to be able to say: "Why?" I mean we say: "Why?" but we're still taking in like a sponge whatever from our parents, our grandparents or whoever raised us.

For example, I tend to be coaching a lot of people who went to boarding school. There's a lot of stuff happening around there because they had significant other people raising them who were tough. I'm coaching a lot of people with sexual abuse. I remember one man who said: "What clients do you get?" I said: "I get a lot of boarding school and sexual abuse." He put up both his hands and said: "Which one do you like?" He ended up loving the coaching so much, he became a student. He came and learned all the material.

That must be very rewarding when that happens.

That happens a lot. I say: "What do you really want to do with your life?" They say: "I want to do what you do." I say: "Then let me show you how." I think everyone should be doing what they want to do, not what they think they should do.

Let me give you an example. I went into a car dealership once. I was going to train the staff and I said to the lady: "What's all this stuff on the wall that you've got here?" She said: "That's all the other car dealerships. That's how they went this month. I said: "Why would you need to know that?" She said: "We need to know how everyone's going." I said: "No, you don't. Do you know the bottom 95% of the population all need to know how somebody else is going? The top 5% of the population that earn 95% of the world's income, they don't give a stuff about what other people are doing. They are so busy creating what they're doing, that other people have to compete to keep up with them. You're spending all this energy on what other people are doing. Imagine if you could take all this energy and just put it into what you can create for yourself as a car dealership, so that you're doing something different to every other car dealership. You're the one that's going to be at that top 5%, not the other companies."

So be a pioneer.

I think that's one of those keys that you were looking for. Create. Go create. We don't have to compete with anyone. We just need to create. You know, we are creative beings.

Yes, but people kind of forget that along the way.

Absolutely, because how many people have been told: "We don't believe that. You're too cheeky. Speak when you're spoken to." Those things still come up as adult if somebody hasn't – like me – helped to change them.

Now if somebody wanted to just leave their job tomorrow, do you think it's wise if they do some reading first? For example, *Rich Dad, Poor Dad* or one of those types of books? Do you think it's a good idea to phase in a dual life, if you like? What's your opinion on that?

I think there are opportunities for both. For me, when I was at Royal North Shore Hospital, I just cut the cords and said: "No, I don't want to work for somebody else any more. I'm going to go out and I'm going to create." However, I was fortunate because I was with my husband of 20 years at that time and he was earning an income. So in a way, I was blessed that there was an income coming in for me to have that time to experiment. So I have to be truthful about that and be realistic.

When I was on my own and I was working at a place that I didn't want to work at any more, to cut the cords and move on, I gradually moved myself into part-time work at the place I was at, and I moved myself into another part-time. I started setting up a consultancy around T.A.F.E. [Teaching & Further Education colleges] and universities because I became quite a guru for information. So I thought, 'well, why not teach if that's what I want to do?' That's when the T.A.F.E colleges and the universities started to pick me up. You can make enormous amounts of money and I thought, 'well, let's start teaching other people.' That was a gradual process where you gradually fade out, but it didn't take me long to let it go.

The same thing happens when I'm in business. I set up a sports camp situation for the last 14 years for children in the school holidays. Why was that important? Because I knew that if I can't affect the parents, I can affect the children and children will teach parents beautifully. Kids could come to me and say: "I don't want to play baseball because I don't know how." I'd say: "Why don't you come, learn and *when*," so it's all NLP language, "*when* I show you how to hit the ball on the other side of the oval, why don't you have a go?" They say: "I'd love to." All of a sudden, from not wanting to play a sport because they didn't know how, to be able to go home and having a homerun under their belt was very different.

More information at: www.lynda-dyer.com

TWELVE

Susan Sly

Susan Sly is a successful entrepreneur, speaker, trainer, athlete and nutritional consultant with over 17 years' experience in health and fitness. She's overcome many trials and tribulations in her life including divorce, bankruptcy and illness. She's generated over $50 million sales in networking marketing and is a seven-figure annual earner. She's author of the bestselling book, *Have It All Woman*.

Q. Susan, you've got two businesses, tell me a little about these and how you came to set them up.

Like many people out there, I grew up with this mindset that you went to school, you got a good job and then that would be it. However, even though that was what my father was telling me do, he and my grandmother ran a restaurant. So I grew up in our family business and

I saw them working very, very hard. My grandmother would start at five in the morning, she'd go straight through to eleven. My dad would start a little bit later at about ten and he's go until two in the morning. I saw them work, work, work and have these employees. But I also saw that they were in charge and there was part of me that thought: 'I can't be an employee. I'm just psychologically not employable.'

What happened was I started to pursue different business ventures. I started my first business when I was eleven. I started making Christmas ornaments and selling them to the customers at the restaurant. Then when I was in my early twenties, I became a personal trainer and a nutritionist. I started a business, then I purchased a health club.

I remember the Queen many, many years ago talking about her *annus horribilis*, and I believe that we all have those times. So for me it was the year 2000. I was rundown and my doctor thought it was just stress. I thought, 'Really, there's something more to this' and he was just like: "Go on vacation." I went on vacation and it didn't help, I actually felt worse. I was exhausted and I was dropping things. At times I wasn't able to think what I wanted to say, the words wouldn't come out of my mouth. So I went back to him and I said: "You come to me for your nutritional advice. You come to me when you want to know what to do with your training. I'm coming to you and I really want these tests done because there's something that's not quite right."

So on January 13th, he called me into his office and said, "Susan, you have multiple sclerosis. You have lesions all over your brain, and within 10 years you'll be in a wheelchair." I was devastated because I was in my twenties and I was a mom. Suddenly my whole life flashed before me and I thought, 'this really isn't what I signed up for in life. I still have unrealised dreams, I have all these goals.'

Three days later, I was on the computer researching MS and I found a chat log from my then husband. He was having an affair. That all happened within three days and I knew I had to step back a little bit. My husband had been the one making the business decisions for our health club and I was the one doing the promoting and the marketing, organising the class schedule, teaching classes and things.

It wasn't long after that that I ended up getting even more ill and coming down with adrenal burn-out. My thyroid went very, very low. I ended up with shingles as well. I had been in the United States racing: I was a competitive athlete at that time and I had my elite status for duathlon and triathlon. I actually fainted on television, on ESPN. I thought, 'here are my minutes of fame, that's it.' When I came back to Canada, I had to do a lot of soul searching and recuperation. A friend of mine said to me: "Susan, you define yourself so much by owning a Mercedes, you own this health club and you have a weekly talk show, you write these articles and you're on television. But if you lost everything tomorrow, if you had no family, no money, nothing, who would you really be?" The truth was I didn't know the answer to that.

So I went out on my bike. I went for a long ride and I really thought about it. In a lot of prayer and meditation a word came to me, and the word that came to me was 'teacher'. It was an incredible moment because even though I was teaching at universities and colleges, guest lecturing and doing these things, I knew it didn't mean 'teacher' in that traditional sense. I believed that the most powerful teachers in the world are those who teach from a place of integrity because they've been in those situations. They're not just talking about situations, they have actually gone through the journey. It wasn't long after that that I went in to my health club to teach a class in the morning and there was a padlock on the door. We'd been shut down and we were tens of thousands of dollars in debt for back taxes, and I didn't realise that it had come to that.

I made several decisions in that moment: 1. That I couldn't stay with a person who was not being faithful in a marriage; 2. That whatever it took, I would make a commitment to get out of that situation and spend the rest of my life empowering women. I actually went home and I prayed on it and I said: "God, I don't know how this is going to be, but show me the way and I'll do the work." I was exhausted at the time and I was so ill; 3) I decided never again would I ever let someone control my finances and I wouldn't let someone control any of these things that mattered in my life.

Really that was that moment that I took a hundred percent responsibility for my life, and I didn't play the victim card. I didn't say: "Poor me I have MS; poor me I'm a single mom now; poor me my husband wasn't faithful in our marriage." Even though it was really hard, I knew that I couldn't be a victim.

So I found myself going to Toronto and taking a job for the largest health club chain in the world at that time, in management, and working really hard. When I first got to Toronto, I didn't have a place to live, I didn't have any money, I was over $100,000 in debt. I ended up living on my brother-in-law's sofa. Through a chain of events that brought me to that health club, I ended up going into a women's business meeting and meeting a woman there who became my client. This woman introduced me to direct sales and network marketing. She taught me the right way to do things. She introduced me to books like *Rich Dad, Poor Dad* and *Think and Grow Rich* and so many other books. One of the things I thought was these books were all written by men, and I put that as a sidebar to myself. I kept thinking, 'this notion of residual income is so amazing for women and so liberating. If I had had this when I went through everything else, my *annus horribilis*, things would have been so different.'

So she groomed me much like one would groom a thoroughbred horse. Even though that first company we were in wasn't the right fit, and we went to a couple of other companies, I found out what I didn't want. I got to work and became a millionaire.

As a sidebar to that, in my successes I was very blessed to meet a person who ran seminars. He said: "You really need to go and take your message to more people." My big joke is if one can stand up as a fitness instructor in front of 50 people in a thong leotard and motivate them, then you can do it as a speaker in front of thousands of people. I had been speaking for years and I have done corporate speaking events for different companies.

So I thought about it, and that's why I ended up launching my programme Step Into Your Power because I felt that the majority of our target audience is women and women entrepreneurs, and not necessarily just from the industry of direct sales. It could be people who own their own businesses: they do accounting from home, they're a seamstress from home, they're doing something that is providing another stream of income for the family. So that really has been a passion. From there, many of the dreams that I've had have become realised. One of the things I'm passionate about is our women's weekend. In that weekend, we have women that come and we focus on relationships and personal health: falling deeply and madly in love with one's own self, how to get your head on straight and how to achieve balance. How one person achieves balance, it's not the same as how another person achieves balance. So, we're looking at that and allowing women to find a space that really works for them. We're helping women heal their relationships, create more self love, more positive outcomes, create more money in their lives.

My vision is to take that event all over the world. Currently, we're doing that in Canada and we're doing our first US event. It's an event that I feel strongly about taking to the UK and also to Australia. So, that's how it was all born and I have a vision to massively impact the lives of a million women on the planet. I'm living into that through all of the different work that I do. I believe very strongly that when a woman is empowered and she feels good about herself, then she's a better mother and she's a better lover and she's more adept in her business, and that's really exciting.

We're living in a brilliant time when we have many powerful female role models. Even though there's still a glass ceiling out there, there are women who are breaking new ground all the time. It used to be that women were merely the trophy wives and had the positions because they were heading different charitable causes. That's lovely and it is very, very important. But now we're seeing women in business and we're seeing women who are helming countries. We're seeing women in massive positions in power. I was just recently in Malawi and doing some interviews there and had the privilege to connect with Joyce Banda who's the Vice President of Malawi. She is considered the most powerful woman in Africa. That is really a patriarchal society, yet she is a woman who can get things done. So there is lots of evidence that women are breaking new ground, but we still have a lot of work to do.

You've mentioned role models and having a mentor. How important do you think that is for your success and for other women's success?

It's hugely important. Mentors can take different forms. There are a lot of women who say: "Susan, I really don't know anyone. My social circle, my family circle, they are very negative. They don't understand why I'm pursuing my dreams." So, read a book, read a biography. That's why I wrote, *Have It All Woman*. Read books like this one, these stories of uplifting fulfilment. I have been very blessed to share the stage with both Jack Canfield and Mark Victor Hansen who wrote the *Chicken Soup for the Soul* books. Buy those books. You can go online, you can go on television and see the biographies of incredible women. If you are fortunate enough, get out to events, find these women who are doing what you want to do. Call them up and say: "May I take you for lunch, may I take you for tea? I want to interview you. Can I ask you some questions? I want to know what books you read, what your daily schedule looks like. How do you get through those wall-kicking times?"

For me, my first mentor in our industry was a woman and I'm very grateful to her – she trained me very, very well. Sometimes your mentors come in for a season and they leave. You don't want to be sad, you just want to step into this place of gratitude and say: "I'm so grateful for what they taught me. The universe is providing me now with someone new." So from there, I went on to have a couple of male mentors. I then found a woman who had been the top income earner at three separate companies and was at the helm of a direct selling company and she became my mentor. So, I continue to have mentors.

This year, I sat down with Mark Victor Hansen. He is such a mega bestselling author. He's the only person to ever have a fiction and a non-fiction book on the *New York Times* bestselling list on the same week. So I sat down with Mark, I consider him a mentor. I'm working on a new project, a new book. So he was giving me some guidance. So sometimes a mentor doesn't have to come in to your life for years, it might just be for 25 minutes, it might be for 15 minutes – people can impact your life with even a brief encounter. For a few years consecutively, I did events with Jim Rohn. Mr. Rohn is incredible, a beautiful business philosopher, so spiritual and so peaceful. Jim Rohn was the personal coach to Anne Geddes, the photographer, and he's brilliant. It would just be one or two little things he said, I would take those things and apply those things. Even though I don't have a personal relationship with Jim, I've done events where when I'm speaking he's speaking. I do consider him a mentor.

So a mentor can also be someone you don't have a personal relationship with, who is at a level that you want to be at. But the bottom line in mentorship is when they say something, don't think about it, don't hypothesise 50 million different outcomes, just do it. One of my mentors asked me to do things that I was nervous to do – just to call people out of the phonebook, going up and talking to people on the street. I was nervous to do that. But he was making the kind of income that I wanted to make, so I did it and became very proficient at that. Then I had another mentor who told me to run ads and do those kinds of things. So I ran the ads and I was nervous, but then I got really good at it and I signed people up into my business from that. So, a mentor will tell you something that may scare you. But if that mentor is coming from a place where they have been there and they've done that and they've had those experiences, then just surrender, just do it. This emotional resistance that we have at times is what keeps us stuck, and it's exhausting. You're never going to get ahead if you don't break these fears down. The only way to do that is to get out and have those experiences for yourself.

What sort of staff support do you have to drive your business forward? Do you have a strong team behind you?

I have two full-time staff and then one part-time staff member. My husband, Chris, who is my great love, I met him when I was 13. As I said: sometimes we have to know what we don't want, to know what we do want. We re-met when I had my *annus horribilis*. He was a chartered accountant and he worked with the world's largest accounting firms. Now we work together in both of our businesses and it's a wonderful life.

You mentioned at one point you were $100,000 in debt. How did you get past that hurdle emotionally and psychologically?

When you're in that level of debt, with no job, it feels very much like being at the bottom of the well and someone is shovelling sand into it. You just have that weight on your chest, which I had for several years. When I looked at the debt, I decided to break it down. So, what does $100,000 in debt look like? It looks like 100,000 single dollars. So knowing that and breaking it down into those bite-sized pieces made it a lot easier.

For years and years, my career was to help people transform their bodies. I worked with difficult cases, people who were 100 pounds or more overweight. I would say: "Don't focus on that level of weight. That's like banging your head against the wall. Focus on five pounds at a time, just the smallest amount." When they did that, they were able to get the weight off. When they focused on all of it at one time, it was very tough.

The same thing is true now – and for years we did life coaching – that when someone has that level of debt, you just break it down into those small pieces. In my life what I do is I have the big goals, they're out there in the peripheral. However, I'm always looking at, 'what is the next step, what is the next step?' In the movie, *The Secret*, Jack Canfield says you can drive from LA to New York which is thousands of miles. But truthfully, if you have the headlights on, you only need to see the next 200 feet, and I live my life that way. I have this vision to empower a million women all over the world, yet I'm just always focused on the next woman. So I have visions of how much money that I want to generate, but I'm always focused on what is that next level.

Really, as women, we can focus on things that seem too far away. Let's say you never made a million dollars a year, the most you made for instance was £25,000 a year and you decide you want to make a million pounds a year – or euros – it seems so far away because you're just chemically not programmed for that yet. So you want to focus on getting to that next level, that next increment and then growing and going from there forward. So that's what I do in all things in my life. We just recently had a baby, and it was baby number four. So, I didn't say: "I want to be a size four" right out of the delivery room. Perhaps Posh can do that – I don't know how she does it – and look fabulous. She can just walk out and look like she belongs on the cover of *Vogue*. But what I did is I just focused on the next five down, and the next five down, and the next five down, and the next five down until I got it, as opposed to saying: "My goodness, I walked out of the delivery room and I was three sizes away from my normal size." So, focusing on breaking the big goal down to smaller goals, that's the key to achieving any task.

You mentioned that you're a mother of four children – ranging from a newborn to twelve years. How do you manage to combine family life with business life?

We get asked that all the time. The first thing I would say is that I'm always in the moment. Like any person who's a parent, we have moments. There's these moments when: "No, I don't want to eat my veggies" and there's moments when: "No, I don't want to wear that sweater." My children were previously in schools that had uniforms and now they're not. If you're reading this and your child is in a school with uniform, just count that as one of your blessings on your 'gratitude list'! So we have those moments, and I just breathe and I take it one moment at a time.

I also have a very set schedule, so I do business when my three older children are in school. When they come home which is four o'clock, I'm focused on family time. From four o'clock until eight-thirty when they go to bed, that's family time when they're going through lessons and we're doing homework. We always sit down and have dinner as a family. When we do that – and this is something anyone can implement – we always say: "What were your high points today? What are you grateful for today?" So everyone goes around and shares something they're grateful for. Then we do it before bed when our children pray, and I say: "What are you grateful for?" They say that in their prayers. So we're constantly connecting with them, checking in, finding their perspective. Chris and I as parents, we're also very quick to have clearing conversations with our children and saying: "Yesterday when you were upset, Mummy could have handled that better and I'm really sorry." So we are quick to have those conversations because we're raising our children to be the future leaders of tomorrow.

What sort of challenges do you think that women face in business or as entrepreneurs? Do they face different challenges to men or similar ones?

Well, different for sure. Women, we're just wired differently. A good friend of mine is Dr. John Gray who wrote *Men are from Mars and Women are from Venus,* and John is lovely. He talks about the neuro-connections for men and for women. Essentially for women, we have way more neuro-pathways between our left and right brain, so our emotional brain and our logical brain. As a result of this, women have a hard time making logical decisions that are not attached to emotions. Even something as innocuous as going to the grocery store, we think, 'Okay, if I go to the grocery store and it takes 45 minutes, and then I have to run here and I have to run there, then I'll get home five minutes late. That will affect my ability to get the homework done.' So, we're constantly thinking like this. At times for us, it's a constant chatter that goes on in our minds, it's endless.

I have a joke where I say: "Women have the ability to make love, plan a week's worth of meals, plan the holiday for next year, figure out where their children are going to go see a university and know what they're going to wear on New Year's Eve five years down the road, and they can do it all at one time." That's us, right? So then you add a business into the mix, and these decisions that should be logical – for instance connecting with three potential clients – it becomes very emotional. "What if they say no? What if they reject me? What if they think that I'm not good enough to lead them?" On and on and on, so it's this battle that goes in between the logical and the emotional brain. We have that innately to protect our children, because if we didn't we would be able to walk out the door and say: "Just go fend for yourself, you're five months old."

Men have fewer neuro-connections and they have that because they're designed to be the protector, the hunter and gatherer. They make a decision filled by testosterone and they can just follow through. Whereas for us, we're always thinking about cause and effect and the consequences. Men just don't think that way. So when it comes to business, a man tends to have a thicker skin when it comes to things, in general, and I know men who are very connected with both their emotional self and their logical self. But when it comes to business, a man is able to have rejection and just go: "So what buddy, it doesn't matter what you think. Next." Whereas women are like: "I've got to rescue that person. I've got to explain to them. I'm so embarrassed that they rejected me. I'm going to send them flowers." That's us.

So the challenge for women is that we do have to access our logical brain in order to make millions of dollars. I have to do this by myself as well. I was raised by my dad so I'm very able to do that and to understand that level of thinking which is just that 'high production, doing business, not getting attached'. When I feel that my more feminine energy is coming in and I feel emotional around decisions, I go out for a walk or I'll take a little break. I'll reconnect with myself, go to the gym just to re-centre myself. That's why it's more of a challenge for us as women. However, women do make masterful entrepreneurs because we're able to naturally connect and share and really have a desire to help people.

An entrepreneur, in order to be super-successful, has to see a problem and have a strong desire to fill that problem. So, Bill Gates, as an example, he saw that there wasn't really a computer-operating system that everyone could understand. So he designed Windows and became one of the wealthiest men in the world. Then even J.K. Rowling – who's absolutely just one of my sheroes – her story and how many people rejected her book on and on and on. She had a vision of entertaining a certain group of people, and she created this boy wizard – of course that really transcended a larger audience. You have young children who read those books and you have people who are into their nineties who read *Harry Potter*. She filled that gap and had a strong desire to really touch people's lives with this story. As a result, she became one of the wealthiest women in the world.

Even Oprah is another prime example where she saw what was missing from people's lives – women had stopped reading, and now she has them reading the classics. Apparently Oprah has had a greater impact on book sales than any other person on the planet because if she endorses a book, everyone buys it. So it really and truly can be a women's world with entrepreneurship, but women are going to have to access their logical brain and let go of being attached. You are going to face rejection, you are going to face apathy from people, you are going to face attrition, people are going to come and go out of your life. You are going to face times when you really question: "Should I keep on forging on?" I cannot tell you one successful entrepreneur I know that didn't have an *annus horribilis* or didn't have several of those before they got to the other end where they started to see enough success to keep them going.

Your mission is to empower individuals, to transcend any barriers holding them back from greatness. What would you say is the single, biggest barrier that holds people back?

The biggest thing that I would say holds people back from greatness – and especially if we're thinking about women – is this battle that we do emotionally and spiritually. It's: "What will happen if I'm successful, what will the consequences be?" I had a woman, my neighbour, I helped her lose over a hundred pounds, and her friends became so critical. That is a prime example. She was over a hundred pounds over her healthy weight, her cholesterol was up and her blood pressure was up. She said: "My friends didn't care about me then, but when I got healthy, that's when they decided to get angry." So as women we'll think about, 'If I become successful, will I lose my friends? What will happen to my family?' We have this notion that we can't make millions of dollars without being away from our family. No, that's not the case, you can do it. You absolutely can do it.

So we're always living into this, 'My gosh, what will the negative outcome be of our success' as opposed to, 'What will the positive income be? Wow, I'll have more time with my family, I'll have more choices. We'll be able to travel the world and my children will be able to have a global education. I will be able to retire with my partner and we can be at home together. That will be lovely, it will be empowering. Yes, by the way, in order for me to become successful, I'm going to help a lot of other people become successful. I'm going to create more economy. I'm going to create more money in households. I'm going to help a lot of other women.' Living in the negative outcomes is the biggest thing that holds us back, as opposed to living in the positive outcomes.

Even for myself, as I think going to that next level, it doesn't have to mean more time away from my family because I'm thinking bigger. I'm going to think, 'Wow, if I want to take *Have It All Women* to different places, then I'll just bring my family with me and it will be a wonderful, wonderful thing to do.' So, thinking differently, and much more globally because money allows us to have a lot more choice and freedom.

If someone came to you today in a similar position to you back in 2000 – heavily in debt, with illness, no kind of emotional support because they just got divorced – what advice would you give them? If they have to take a step tomorrow, one step, to turn their lives around what would it be?

It's a great question. Know this, that everything really and truly does happen for a reason. Often, to be triumphant, we have got to be broken down so that when the pieces are put back together they're even more magnificent. When one looks at any successful person, any person who's been triumphant, let's look at Nelson Mandela, how many years did he spend in prison and I can't imagine what that would be like. Any person with great success has got to have those tribulations. So wherever a person is at right now, know that it may be challenging, it may be frustrating, you may not see the light at the end of the tunnel, but know that it is all perfect because really and truly we are the authors of our own success story.

So if they have to break down the steps that they need to take – say for example finding a mentor, educating themselves – what would the principle ones be?

Number One, no matter where you're at, set goals, set big goals. I have a goal book that's got 1,500 goals in it. When you're a little girl, you daydream, 'I want to be a princess; I want to ride off on a white horse; I want to be the queen; I want to marry a Prince William.' Start dreaming. Start writing goals down no matter how silly you think they are, even if you still want to be a princess. My second youngest daughter, she is convinced she's going to be a princess. She tells us: "I'm going to be a princess." She wears princess dresses. She wanted to wear a tiara in school. Absolutely, we are not a royal family. However, there are many opportunities for her if she wants to be a princess or she can create her own country and become the monarch there.

Keep dreaming, write those goals down. Don't stop. Challenge yourself, just write a hundred to start and dream big. Keep it in a special book wherever you can see it. You don't have to know the 'how', you just have to know the 'what'. The universe takes care of the 'how'.

Number Two is be grateful now and start in gratitude, that's a different attracting energy. So start with being grateful for perhaps the sun shining or your child laughing or whatever it is, maybe a lovely phrase you saw, a book you read. Start with gratitude.

One of the people I mentor, they send me their list of 10 items every day to be accountable. Find an accountability partner and say: "Let's send each other our 10 items of gratitude every single day."

The third thing is begin to share your dreams with other people, because I believe we're only three people away from that person who can make our next level of our dream come true. I've tested this theory time and time again in my workshops. I'll say: "Tell me someone you'd like to meet" and someone might say President Obama. Well, I happen to be friends with a woman whose husband is one of the primary guards for President Obama, that's an easy one. Someone will say "Oprah" and you'll hear someone in the audience say: "My friend used to be an intern on that show but is still good friends with the executive producer, I could get you to Oprah." So we're only three degrees of separation away, the more people you tell and begin to share, that's when the magic is going to happen because people say: "Hey, I actually know someone" or "I know how you can do that." So, that will all be presented in front of you.

Then the fourth step is to act. Don't sit there, you've got to act. So, all of these opportunities are going to start appearing for you and all these great people, but if you don't take action then you're going to stay stuck. Acting is hard. However, 90% of what we fear never comes true, only 10% of what we fear comes true. Just know that and put yourself out there.

The last thing I will say is play the contribution game. Even in The Bible, in Deuteronomy, it says when you give you'll get back a thousand fold. Not even ten-fold – a thousand-fold. It doesn't have to be money, just play the contribution game. You can go into the pub for instance, you can just buy someone a drink, and they don't even know you. You can bring in someone's newspaper for them. You can help someone cross the street. You can do something, start to play the contribution game and watch how life just turns from black and white to technicolour as things start to come back to you and you can have a lot of fun with that.

So, those would be the steps that I would recommend you take. And stay plugged in. Read books and attend conferences, and do those things to really charge you up. If you take your mobile phone but you never plug it in, the charge is only going to be good for just the life of that battery. The same is true of us, we've got to constantly recharge ourselves because our batteries are going run out, especially us women.

So we've got to replug in so that recharges us again, so we can go out and do the great things that we're meant to do.

You mentioned your notebook of goals. Do you have any other rituals every day? Do you have a vision board with pictures of your goals on it, or do you meditate? What sort of things do you do on a day-to-day basis?

I have all of it. I have a vision board that I'm looking at right now. I have different things in my office: I have my goals up on big sheets of paper on my walls. Every night I do 10 items of gratitude. I write my day in advance even though I keep a paper planner. I keep a spiral notebook and my assistant jokes she can sell them on eBay and make a fortune. The night before I always write what I'm going to be doing on the day in advance. I'm a very visual learner, I'm a kinaesthetic learner. So, I write these things out. Those are just some of my rituals. I make sure every day I get some form of exercise. I drink plenty of water every day, at least 12-15 glasses. I make sure I take really good nutritional products.

I always start my day with the same prayer which is: "God, please help me to be the best wife I can be. Please help me to be the best mother I can be. Please help me to touch and move and inspire everyone you put in my path." So, I start my day in prayer, end my day in prayer, always start and finish in gratitude.

What drives you? What do you enjoy most about your work and what motivates you every day?

Change. Knowing that I've made a difference, knowing that my assistance could matter in the life of another – whether it's a little child who is in Malawi who we take to a clinic, or a woman who's struggling to get her business off the ground and we help her really figure that out; a woman perhaps who's in a marriage with someone she's deeply in love with but they've lost that ability to communicate and it's hard and everyone's feeling it, and we assist her. So all of those things drive me and motivate me.

You're involved in a fundraising project supporting girls rescued from brothels in Cambodia, tell me a little about this.

The project is helmed by World Vision. Sex trafficking is a massive problem in the world. In a place as poor as Cambodia, it is actually an industry. This is shocking a lot of people, but it's not openly discouraged for girls to enter this as a line of work. Especially with the recession many factories closed down, and we saw a lot of women going to the massage parlours and brothels to work voluntarily. However, not all girls and boys who are there are of their own volition, so there are children raised by different Non-Government Organisations. When the children are taken from the brothels, they're given the opportunity to go into a programme that will allow them to develop skills and get an education and a trade. For those who would like to do that – though some prefer to go back into the sex trade, believe that or not – there are programmes that help them do that. Unfortunately the programmes are very expensive and very difficult to get funding for. World Vision offers one such programme and it's at a place called Niva Thmeay. The Cambodia Trauma Centre has these girls. You can have four-year-old girls in there. The first time I visited, there were sisters, four and five, who had been brutally repeatedly raped, just abandoned by their primary family. Then you might have girls who are 13 or 14 who are working in the brothels because it's a great way to make money. But they decided they don't want to do that any more, so you have the whole spectrum.

One of the girls I interviewed there, her parents sold her in the virgin auction. She was forthcoming about being there as a five-year-old girl and her traumas – she was purchased by a Westerner – and she talked about what goes on and so on and so forth.

So these girls have a wonderful life there where it's a safe environment and a healthy environment. So, my husband Chris and I are avid supporters of it and we work very hard to raise awareness for it. To run this centre, just at the bare minimum, it takes about $400,000 a year. There's several people contributing to that project through World Vision. Truthfully, the biggest group of people who are keeping the sex trade going are the European and North American men. I think it's something that even though we may be on the other end of the world, we all have a responsibility to assist these children.

How did you get involved in that project?

I had a personal development seminar and the person leading it, who's a good friend of ours, said: "Think of a goal that's worthy of your life. Just shout it, don't put a lot of thought to it." So I stood and I said: "I'm going to free the world of child prostitution." I didn't know how I was going to do this, it's such a big problem. Initially, I just felt that someone had punched me in the stomach and I'm thinking: "Goodness, how am I going to do this?" I thought, 'I'm not even going to worry about the 'how' I'm just going to put that goal out there.'

A year later, because Chris and I had sponsored 20 children through World Vision, we were contacted and asked what it was that we were interested in, so I shared what I was interested in. They told me about the trauma centre and I arranged to go and visit it. I just fell in love with the girls, fell in love the team there, the staff. So, I do try to go over there once a year, and I was just there several months ago. This is one of the most incredible places on earth.

That's how I got involved. I'm working, albeit so quickly, on a new book called *Interrupted Wishes*, which will be written in fiction about the plight of girls in the sex trade. The reason I've chosen to do it as fiction is because a lot of the non-fiction, with regards to this topic, is so graphic that people have a hard time digesting that this is the truth of what happens. But for some reason it's more palatable as a fiction piece. I interviewed eight girls when I was there the last time. It allowed me to take their different stories and draft them into this main character. That's what I'm doing and it's a labour of love, and then the proceeds of the book will go to the trauma centre.

More information at: www.StepIntoYourPower.com